Multinational Corporations and National Elites:

A Study in Tensions

By Joseph LaPalombara and Stephen Blank

A Research Report from The Conference Board's
Division of Public Affairs Research
Walter A. Hamilton, Vice President

Highlights for the Executive

MULTINATIONAL CORPORATIONS AND NATIONAL ELITES: A STUDY IN TENSIONS *by Joseph LaPalombara and Stephen Blank* · Report No. 702

T HIS STUDY examines U.S. multinational corporate behavior in Canada and Italy, countries illustrative of advanced industrial nations. It also explores extensively the attitudes, expectations and perceptions of corporate behavior of public and private sector leaders in those countries who have substantial influence both on public opinion and public policy.

The fieldwork for this study involved 190 open-ended and focused interviews with 247 persons in three categories: (1) headquarters, regional and local affiliate managers of participating multinational firms operating in Canada and Italy; (2) officials of the U.S. government located in the United States, Canada and Italy; and (3) Canadian and Italian officials, leaders and decision makers drawn from government, political parties, central and regional administrative agencies, the mass media, trade unions, academic and intellectual circles, and the indigenous business and industrial communities.

The study is divided into four parts. Part One introduces the problem, summarizes some findings, pinpoints the major questions asked, and provides background material (including some basic data on Canada and Italy) against which the findings should be assessed and interpreted. Part Two refers to those aspects of U.S. multinational operations in Canada and Italy that are seen as relating to general problems of society, and of economic and industrial development. These chapters treat the broad overall perceptions and judgments of Canadians and Italians about foreign (particularly U.S.) direct investment in their respective countries.

Part Three centers on a number of problems that are closely related to the operational side of American multinational affiliates in the countries studied. The list of problems is not exhaustive; it is not meant to cover every conceivable operating problem that U.S. firms encounter overseas.

Part Four deals with the future. It incorporates possible and probable future policy developments overseas that directly involve or affect American industrial enterprise abroad, as well as possible future developments in Western Europe, and alternative patterns of multinational organization.

Contents

Tables

Acknowledgments

Fieldwork was greatly facilitated by valuable assistance provided by many persons and organizations. Dr. Donald Guertin of the Exxon Corporation served as a senior research consultant from the beginning and contributed substantially both to the study design and to the execution of the research itself. In Canada we had the assistance of the offices of The Conference Board in Canada, and particularly the extensive and understanding assistance of Dr. Arthur Smith, former president of The Conference Board in Canada. In Italy, interviews with the industrial community and with other leaders were facilitated through the good offices of the Research and Cultural Affairs Department of the Fiat Corporation, a Conference Board Associate. We are indebted to Dr. Luigi Ferro, Dr. Mario Ponti, and Dr. Francesco Caposio of that department for the remarkable efficiency and goodwill that went with their help. The Center of Mediterranean Studies at Rome—its director, Mr. E.A. Bayne, and its able staff—provided office space, secretarial assistance, and generally served as a base of operations in Italy. Dr. Giovanna Pennacchi and Dr. Paolo Zannoni arranged individual appointments and generally kept the work schedule within manageable bounds. Finally, we wish to express our thanks to Mr. Herman Burdick, Director of the American Chamber of Commerce in Italy, for enabling us to meet with a number of members of the American business community there.

We are also deeply obligated to all of those who agreed to be interviewed, and we thank them as a group in order to hold to our agreement that they would remain anonymous. Similarly, our study of corporate decision making regarding overseas affiliates could not have proceeded without the willing assistance of top-level managers in the participating firms. Ten major American corporations gave us an astonishing amount of time—and of open collaboration—in the United States, in Canada, in Italy, and in European regional offices where they exist.

Mr. Michael Johnson and Mr. Herbert Meyers of the Office of Private Cooperation (Department of State) provided encouragement, early critiques of the research design, and a wide range of other help.

Elizabeth Hanson helped with the interviews in Canada and Robert Black assisted in the preparation of the final manuscript. Heliena Colorafi and Selma Mackler provided able and understanding secretarial support. At a critical moment in the whole process, we had the expert assistance of Constance LaPalombara.

J. LaPalombara
S. Blank

Foreword

THE BEHAVIOR of multinational corporations in the countries in which their subsidiaries or affiliates operate has become a matter of increasing concern to both business and government and their publics. This study deals with the U.S. multinational corporation in advanced industrial nations. It is part of a larger effort by the Board to examine responsible corporate behavior overseas. The study's central thrust is to delineate important factors that are associated at home and abroad with such behavior. It provides perspective for those public and private sector executives who have policy and operational responsibilities for managing overseas affiliates.

The factor explored most extensively in this report is the attitudes and expectations of strategic elites in two countries—Canada and Italy—regarding the American corporate affiliate. Other factors considered are the internal decision-making structure of the multinational firm and the relationships between the U.S. multinational firm at home and abroad and agencies of the U.S. government. The study provides an indication of future developments in advanced industrialized nations in which American capital is directly and indirectly invested.

Both Canada and Italy have the forms of industrial enterprise (including their own multinationals), economic infrastructure, trade union and employer organizations, and public administrative arrangements that conform to a "Western" model. Both are members of the Organization for Economic Cooperation and Development; one is a member of and the other "associated" with the European Communities; and both are involved as "developed" nations playing a role in the Third World. In both countries there is substantial involvement of U.S. firms in the domestic economy, and in both countries the political environment in which U.S. multinationals operate is changing rapidly and extensively. In both countries, the policies and practices of U.S. firms are increasingly subject to criticism by national opinion leaders; in both countries U.S. firms are becoming aware that past definitions and criteria of good corporate citizenship are undergoing significant reevaluation; and in both countries U.S. firms now find it necessary to review their policies and practices in light of these new pressures to determine whether it will be possible to remain active there.

Ten U.S. multinational corporations, representing five industrial areas—chemicals, automotive, pharmaceuticals, hydrocarbons, and electrical and electronic products—cooperated in this study. They reflect the range of U.S. enterprises operating in the more advanced industrial nations of the world. The study began in June, 1975. Extensive fieldwork was carried on between December, 1975 and May, 1976 in the

United States, Italy, Canada and several other nations in Western Europe. The Board is grateful to the Bureau of Education and Cultural Affairs of the State Department for recognizing the significance of this study by partially funding it through a grant from the Office of Private Cooperation.

This study was conducted autonomously by the Board. The report was written by Dr. Joseph LaPalombara, Senior Research Fellow, and Dr. Stephen Blank, Research Associate, with assistance from Elizabeth C. Hanson and Robert A. Black, Jr. This study is the first product of the Multinational Corporate Responsibility Project. The Project is under the general supervision of James F. Harris, Director, Social Responsibility Research.

K. A. RANDALL
President

Part One
The Problem and Its Setting

Chapter 1
Multinationals Under Siege: The Problem

THE MULTINATIONAL corporation is in a state of siege. It is also in a state of moral disorientation and stocktaking. Although the multinational enterprise has been around for over a century, its mushrooming growth in recent years has gained it widespread public attention, much of it unfavorable.

Variations in definitions of what qualifies as a multinational enterprise lead to different estimates as to their number, and the number of affiliates who represent them outside of the parent country. No one contests though that a dozen or so of the leading industrial countries are the home of several thousand multinational corporations whose overseas affiliates number in the tens of thousands.[1]

Most of this enormous proliferation of overseas affiliates, reflecting direct foreign investments by parent companies, occurred in the last one or two decades. Along with this unprecedented expansion has come evidence of dependence of one nation on another, of misbehavior on the part of some corporations, of levels of economic and possibly concomitant political power in the hands of private corporations that many persons find perplexing and unacceptable. In parent and host countries, in national and international political bodies, the cry goes up that the MNC's constitute a major problem—perhaps *the* major problem after war and peace that the world's public authorities must address.

Public authorities are responding. Today it is surely not the sovereign nation-state that is at bay but, rather, the multinational enterprise. In the United States it is the object of extensive public denunciation, demands for stringent regulation, public investigations, and legislative proposals designed to bring this type of economic enterprise to heel. Abroad the MNC encounters similar developments, some of them wryly contradictory. On the one hand, alarms are sounded about the dangers created by economic superpowers that allegedly elude the best efforts of nation-states to control them. On the other hand, even the smallest and seemingly most vulnerable nation-state is discovering and demonstrating how easy it is to use political, legal and administrative instrumentalities to discipline multinational affiliates. These nations are able to extract severe concessions from parent companies; where necessary or opportune, they do not hesitate to drive out the parent company through acts of expropriation or confiscation.

Sir Michael Clapham, a distinguished British statesman and industrialist, has this to say to those who claim that the multinational corporation and the nation-state are today in a state of tension and mutual antagonism:

"Countries may lack the wit or the will to get the most out of multinationals; they certainly do not lack the power to control them. While I would like to think of the

---

[1] In 1973, the United Nations identified 7,276 multinational corporations with headquarters in fifteen countries. The minimum number of affiliates of these firms which could be identified was 27,300. United Nations, *Multinational Corporations in World Development*, ST/ECA/190, 1973, p. 138.

nation-state as an obsolescent form of organization, I have no expectation of its disappearing in the next few centuries: so I hope it will learn to live fruitfully with the multinationals.'' [2]

Sir Michael's hope is fundamental. It is clear that the nation-state is here to stay and that it can and will affect the future of the multinational enterprise. This being so, it is at best really only half the story to argue as some do that because the MNC is the inevitable outgrowth of certain economic imperatives, it is also here to stay. The rest of the story requires that we speculate about where and under what conditions the MNC in the future will continue to wish to locate abroad, and whether these conditions will be acceptable to the nation and government involved.

The study that forms the basis for this report will shed light on this last question. It will suggest why it is precarious to generalize about multinationals and why it makes a lot of sense to look intensively at individual nations that host MNC's. Above all, it will illustrate why it is essential to avoid many abstract preconceptions regarding what is good or bad, right or wrong, about multinationals; what will or will not work abroad; and what kinds of corporate policies and behavior are consistent with the multinationals' desire to continue to be present in foreign countries and markets.

Findings from Canada and Italy

Some of the major general findings from our study of American multinationals in Canada and Italy are:

(1) For developed countries like Canada and Italy, many of the alleged multinational defects so dear to the hearts of MNC critics (and often to those who do research on and write about MNC's) are not widely identified as problems at all. The payment of taxes, product quality, transfer pricing, trade and distribution practices, personnel policies, health and safety practices, land use, training of employees, reinvestment of earnings, and repatriation of profits are *not* primary concerns of host-country elites.

(2) In these countries, elites are generally confident of their ability to ensure that multinational enterprises will conform to the country's legal and administrative requirements. In fact, enforcement is rarely necessary. Where good corporate citizenship refers to strict adherence to a host-country's laws, the affiliates of American MNC's rarely fall below prevailing national standards, and they are frequently exemplars.

(3) In both Italy and Canada, the most frequent criticisms directed at American MNC's have less to do with the MNC as such than with the failures or excesses of governments. Canadians and Italians attack their own governments' inability to develop adequate and efficient regulatory frameworks for MNC's. They also attack the actions of the U.S. government—mainly the extraterritorial application

[2]Sir Michael Clapham, *Multinational Enterprises and Nation States*. London: The Athlone Press, 1975, p. 29.

2

of U.S. law on and through foreign affiliates of U.S. corporations. In fact, in Canada, many feel that U.S. extraterritoriality is the single most serious impediment U.S. firms face in their dealings.

(4) Staffing local affiliate managerial positions with nationals of host countries often creates as many problems as it may solve. In any case, this strategy is not the answer to some very basic feelings about autonomy expressed by Canadians and Italians, including the managers of U.S.-MNC affiliates.

(5) Company codes of conduct, translated into indigenous languages and diffused to the general public of host countries, can be self-defeating. In any event, they are not likely to cut much ice with the critics of U.S. corporate affiliates. Nor are they likely to be emulated by the MNC's of other countries with which U.S. affiliates abroad are forced to compete.

(6) The classic arguments against the decentralization of R and D will find fewer and fewer sympathetic listeners abroad. The question of technology transfer and of assisting host countries to develop their own technologies will be one of the most insistently pressing issues in the years ahead.

(7) Far from lamenting the political involvements and contributions of some American MNC affiliates, Canadian and Italian elites criticize even more the failure of U.S. MNC's in their countries to become more deeply integrated locally, and to develop more acute sensitivity to local feelings, mores, usages.

(8) In both Italy and Canada, elites by and large believe that the further economic development of their countries is dependent upon continued inputs of foreign, and especially American, capital. This view is shared by leading Communist officials in Italy and by many nationalists in Canada.

(9) In both countries, however, it is clear that increasing demands will be made on MNC's to provide greater benefits to host countries, and that conditions governing the activities of MNC's will be not as liberal as in the past.

(10) Most responsible critics of MNC's in these countries do not want them to be forced out, nor do they fail to understand that MNC operations are dependent in the end upon their profitability. What they question, however, is the capacity of the MNC to adapt to changing situations in which the nature of the firm's costs and benefits and how these should be assessed may well be different than in the past.

Taken all together, these and other findings describe a world less hostile to the MNC's than might appear from a reading of the press, the output of academic and intellectual communities in the United States and abroad, or, indeed, the things that American corporate executives themselves have to say about their companies' behavior and future prospects. It is not a benign world, of course, and the rules—as well as the stakes—of the game are changing rapidly for MNC's. But the world, at least of the developed nations, where the far greatest share of MNC activity takes place, is one that seems to be entirely capable of living with international corporate organization.

The point is that the siege facing the MNC's is neither limited to host countries in which they operate nor is it necessarily encountered there in its most aggressive form. In recent months the United States has given ample demonstration that a principal factor—perhaps the critical factor—impinging on the future life and operations of the MNC is the national government of the parent company. Deeply rooted American ambivalence about bigness, and particularly about bigness in business, emerges dramatically in the more recent legislative treatment of the overseas operations of U.S. firms, and in new policy imperatives designed to be much more restrictive of corporate behavior than in the past. Demands for additional governmental controls must be appreciated against the basic understanding that the United States is already in a class by itself regarding the extent to which it prescribes what its corporations (and their overseas affiliates) may or may not do.

International Organizations and the Multinationals

In addition to the national governments of parent companies, international organizations are deeply involved in efforts to establish more stringent regulation and control of MNC's. The report of the United Nations Group of Eminent Persons pointed to a number of problem areas that require attention. The report resulted in the creation of a United Nations Commission on Transnational Corporations. The Commission's Centre on TNC's serves as a research and information center on MNC's. The Centre supports the ongoing efforts of the U.N. Economic and Social Council to develop a code of conduct for MNC's—an effort which has been dominated by the views of the "Group of 77," that is, of the less-developed nations of the world, among whose leaders are found the most outspoken opponents of MNC's.[3]

Efforts by the U.N. to develop a code of conduct for MNC's are unlikely to proceed very rapidly. But other international organizations seem to be making more substantial progress in this direction. The Organization for Economic Cooperation and Development began, early in 1974, to study the functioning of MNC's with a view to the development of a code of conduct for them. By the spring of 1976, a draft code had gained wide acceptance among O.E.C.D. members and advisory business and labor groups. The code was accepted by all 24 O.E.C.D. member countries at the end of June, 1976. It envisages substantial alteration in the international framework for MNC operations, especially in the area of information disclosure, but its essentially voluntary nature sharply distinguishes it from the compulsory code demanded by leaders of the U.N. group.

In the fall of 1972, a meeting of experts convened by the International Labour Organization recommended that the ILO study the possibility of developing social policy guidelines covering MNC operations. A number of research projects and other activities were initiated which by the spring of 1976 resulted in the development of guidelines for a code of conduct dealing with multinational enterprises and social policy, including such matters as employment policies, labor standards, industrial relations, and stability of employment.

International regional organizations have also been active in these areas. Both the European Communities and the Organization of American States have sought

---

[3]The "Group of 77" is a "caucus" of the developing nations formed during "UNCTAD I," a special meeting sponsored by the United Nations Conference on Trade and Development in 1964. It now numbers more than 100 members who take an active interest in international development efforts.

to develop a code of conduct or guidelines that would spell out rules of behavior for MNC's operating in their respective areas. The Commission of the European Communities is also attempting to work out regulations, including an omnibus company law, that would standardize the treatment of MNC's by host countries in Europe.

Public Opinion Abroad and the Multinationals

When we turn to the area of public opinion, a number of important observations are in order. A few years ago, for example, the United States Information Agency conducted a survey of European business executives, high-level civil servants, and professionals on the subject of the role of American business in Western Europe. These were persons possessing a fairly accurate picture of the scope of American investment in their countries; they also, by and large, expected that the level of American investment would increase over the subsequent decade. Indeed, they understood the policies of their own national governments to be encouraging such expansion. In Italy, for example, 71 percent of the 480 persons interviewed by USIA indicated that they considered the national government's policies to be encouraging American business.

In all European countries at the time of this particular survey (1971) most of those interviewed felt that their countries benefited ''at least somewhat'' from the presence of U.S. private investment there. On the other hand, there were countries like Italy, the Netherlands, and Switzerland where upwards of 25 percent of those surveyed considered such investment to be ''somewhat or very harmful.''

When it comes to investments that involve U.S. take-overs, opposition goes up precipitously in most European countries. Indeed, the merger of a number of European companies as an alternative and counterpoise to increased control by U.S. business is overwhelmingly favored by elites throughout Western Europe. The percentage preferring this line of development exceeds 80 percent everywhere except in Norway (66 percent) and Switzerland (69 percent).

The elites surveyed tend to agree that the presence of American business in Europe has introduced more efficiency in local businesses and that a great deal of technical know-how and marketing skills have been transmitted as a result of an American business presence in their respective countries. But between 40 and 70 percent of these elites believe that business independence in their individual countries and throughout Europe is threatened by U.S. investments. They claim further the American firms tend to ignore the locally accepted ways of doing business, and that the growth of international companies carries with it price fixing and other monopolistic practices. Finally, with the exception of Germany and Britain, it is noteworthy that the idea predominates among these elites that the fact of being an international company means that the firms involved can behave as if they were above the law.

More recently, Lloyd Free and his associates have updated information on overseas attitudes toward the United States and toward U.S. business.[4] In their

---

[4]Lloyd Free, *How Others See US; Critical Choices for Americans, Volume III*. Lexington, Mass.: Lexington Books, 1975, pp. 36-7.

worldwide surveys, they asked both elites and general publics how they feel about U.S.-controlled business and industries operating in their countries. In Western Europe, 43 percent of the general public and 49 percent of elites believe that these enterprises benefit the national interest "somewhat" or "a great deal." Those who claim that the opposite is true, that these enterprises are somewhat or greatly harmful, number 30 percent among the general publics and 33 percent among the elites. In the case of Italy, both elites and the public seem somewhat more favorably than unfavorably disposed toward American business. In Canada, where the elites are slightly favorable to U.S. business, the Canadian public is distinctly not so. In fact, the combined average of Canadian elite and general public attitudes places Canada, along with France, in the distinctly hostile category—and considerably more hostile than countries like Britain, Brazil, Mexico and Italy.

The Future of Multinationals

In the face of these misgivings about, and even extreme diffidence toward, the MNC, it is no wonder that there should be demands for greater restrictions and regulations. It is perhaps ironical that these demands should reach a crescendo just as the level of American overseas investment seems to be tapering off.

Many factors go to influence this retrenchment. Expected economic recovery in the United States will make domestic investment both more imperative and more attractive than in the past. So will higher costs of production, more restrictive conditions imposed by host governments, and more uncertain political and economic conditions overseas. But even if, as expected, levels of added U.S. overseas investment fall considerably below what they were in the 1960's and early 1970's, it is predictable that large U.S. financial inputs (probably not under $7 billion annually) will continue to be invested abroad. This conclusion emerges either from the theory that the MNC and its growth follows an *economic* logic and imperative, or from the alternative view that the multinational enterprise is an expression of neomercantilism and, therefore, an instrumentality of the *political* imperatives followed by major world powers like the United States.

Those who lean to the economic explanation of the MNC make forceful arguments that in the years ahead nation-states that wish to develop economically will not be able to get along without the multinationals, that the trend toward the internationalization of economic enterprise is fundamentally irreversible. Even were this the case, however, it does not at all follow that the MNC will in fact be located wherever the need or logic of development might dictate. The forces of economic nationalism and autarchy are already apparent here and there among industrial countries and, indeed, constitute a major factor in countries like Italy and Canada. Furthermore, it is apparent that the MNC of the future will not necessarily assume the form it takes today; similarly, it is not self-evident that the particular MNC's that are dominant in today's world will remain dominant in tomorrow's.

Considerations such as these should arrest the attention of those who direct MNC's, as well as those who are policy makers in MNC home countries. This means particularly that American corporate directors and policy makers should be attentive to developments abroad that affect enterprise. The massive expansion of the multinational enterprise in the last couple of decades has been overwhelmingly an American phenomenon. A committee of the U.N. Secretariat calculated that between 1967 and 1971 the book value of foreign direct investment undertaken by all investor nations increased from $108.2 billion to $165 billion. The U.S. share grew from $59.5 billion to $86 billion, remaining above 50 percent of the total.[5] Today, American direct investment overseas is estimated at more than $120 billion, more than three times the level of the next largest foreign investor, Great Britain. Taken together, the overseas investments of the United States and Great Britain (totaling almost $160 billion) account for about two-thirds of all foreign investments.

In view of the dominant position of the United States in this sphere, it is perhaps inevitable that criticisms of the MNC's and demands that they should be further regulated and controlled, should appear to center on the United States. Our field research, for example, confirms the U.S.I.A. finding that when people think or talk about international firms, they usually mean U.S. companies.

We shall show later that very often it is not merely the dominant position of the U.S. MNC abroad, but also the dominant international position of the United States as a world power that leads to such perceptions. In any event, it is primarily to an American audience that we would address the following question: Given the changing environment confronting the multinational corporation, what is its ability to make those creative adaptations that will permit it to continue to operate abroad in ways consistent with its basic nature and responsibilities as a privately owned enterprise?

The environment referred to is less economic and material than it is political and psychological. It involves a set of perceptions of MNC's, an evaluation of their behavior and utility, and expectations and prescriptions about how they should carry on their activities in a given place at a given time. These environmental factors are important enough when those with whom they are associated are the general public; they become critically important when those referred to are elites—those who, by reason of their positions in the political or economic system or the influence they wield over public policies, can act in ways that directly affect the multinationals.

In other words, one must ask not only what is claimed or said to be good or bad, reassuring or threatening, about multinationals; one must also ask who says these things and with what possible effect if words are turned into policies and actions, particularly the actions of governments. Indeed, it is more important to know who believes, claims or demands what about the MNC's than whether the beliefs and allegations are true, or whether what is demanded is entirely realistic.

Anyone who reads a daily newspaper here or abroad knows that the statements made about the MNC's cover a wide gamut. Sometimes what is said constitutes outlandish horror stories, unsubstantiated by hard evidence; on other occasions we have striking revelations of legally and morally questionable conduct on the part of

[5]United Nations, *op. cit.*, p. 139.

multinational corporate directors at home and abroad. Some persons uncritically describe the MNC as an inherently benign organization whose very existence overcomes national parochialism, furthers international peace, and brings the greatest good to the greatest number on a world scale. Others find the MNC inherently rapacious, deny the validity of the profit motive, insist that the MNC abroad should even operate at a loss as a means of expiating its earlier sins of exploitation, and generally make the MNC the immediate object of more profound ambitions to effect radical transformations of society, polity and economy.

Curiously enough, the MNC is the institution most coveted and most feared by those national leaders who would further economic growth. The fact that the MNC's have neither armies nor guns is not always reassuring. Overbearing political intervention in Chile, as well as the use of large sums of money to win favors from highly placed political and administrative officials in other countries, are events that lead to nightmarish visions of the uses to which economic power can be put. It is then a short step to the conclusion that the MNC is really the instrument of an imperialist national government, available to do whatever bidding those who carry the flag may demand.

Others will take the same information to support the apocalyptic claim that the world will soon be controlled by a few hundred of the largest MNC's. This particular inference reverses the first, for it returns to the idea that national sovereignties are things of the past and that, unless the further development of the MNC's as private centers of economic power is forestalled and cut back, national governments will everywhere be nothing more than corporate pawns.

This last fear persists in the teeth of evidence that national governments are anything but passive actors in their relationships to these economic giants. Again, to cite Sir Michael Clapham:

"Governments have dictated the pattern of ownership; the outflow of revenue and capital; the terms on which inter-company transfers should be made; the remuneration for technology and management; the rate at which expatriates should be replaced by nationals in management; the terms of employment of labour; and, of course, the rate and nature of taxation. They have even forbidden expansion unless and until adequate competition was established. . . . Why then should there be these anxieties about the power of the multinationals?" [6]

The Approach of This Study

The question posed by Sir Michael, as well as others alluded to earlier, requires more research in depth than is possible in the typical study by questionnaire mailed to or administered with large numbers of persons. Many such studies, of widely varying quality, are now available to us. At best, they give us information about who holds what kinds of beliefs or attitudes about MNC's, and perhaps with what degree of intensity. We learn from such studies whether attitudes or clusters of

[6]Clapham, *op. cit.*, p. 22.

them go together, whether these are associated with the age or sex of those surveyed, their religious or political affiliations, their place of residence or degree of contact with foreigners, their education, profession or occupation, and so on.

But these studies rarely give those surveyed the freedom to express themselves in their own words, or to identify the specific topics or problems *they* consider thoughtworthy. Even more rarely do these studies permit us to pick up the nuances that people express when they discuss their beliefs and feelings about MNC's— nuances that then become vitally significant when we try to discover why certain views are held or, more important, what it is people propose and are prepared to do in order to maintain or to change things as they are. We imagine that this particular aspect of interpretation will appeal to readers of this report.

In order to achieve the depth we were after, it was necessary to limit the number of countries in which research was conducted. We decided, in the first place, to concentrate in this phase of our study on the developed countries. (A parallel study which focuses on developing countries is now under way.) Secondly, we chose two countries for examination, Canada and Italy.

We also felt it necessary to secure the cooperation in the project of a limited number of American multinational corporations whose managers we would interview within the parent headquarters, in regional offices where they exist, and in their affiliates located in Italy and Canada. These participating companies are drawn from five different manufacturing categories; in each category we have studied one quite large and one much smaller company. For obvious reasons of confidentiality, neither the companies nor their managers are identified in this report. The relative distribution of company managers and other elites interviewed in this study is given in the Appendix.

We are centrally concerned with these questions:

(1) What is considered to be acceptable and responsible corporate behavior overseas?

(2) Who holds these views, and to what extent are the views consistent and in harmony with each other?

(3) How are U.S. companies operating in the host countries perceived and evaluated by the elites of these countries? Are there significant differences in the degree of accuracy of these perceptions, and the content of the evaluations?

(4) What kinds of prescriptions do these elites lay out for the future, and with what probability that they will turn into real policy or behavior?

It seems to us apparent that, however one may define good corporate citizenship or socially responsible corporate behavior, a variety of structural factors will both influence and limit what the overseas corporate affiliate can do. It is highly unlikely, for example, that a private American corporate affiliate in Italy, whose annual losses are not covered by the public treasury through general redistribution of revenues produced by taxation, can remain in business indefinitely. Yet there are those in Italy who claim that this would be the essence of responsible corporate citizenship. There are consumer and environmentalist groups in both Italy and Canada whose prescriptions regarding what corporations should do to clean up and to protect the environment imply that the corporate community is indeed the national government, with similar capacities and responsibilities.

Structural Factors

We theorized that in our own study three structural factors required close scrutiny. First, we were interested in the relationship between the U.S.-MNC affiliate abroad and a variety of *strategic elites* located in the host countries. These are leading persons drawn from the world of politics and administration, the trade unions, the provincial and regional governments, the mass media, the experts in economics and other intellectual pursuits, and members of the indigenous industrial community, including the managers of the multinational corporations of the host country. They are persons with whom the managers of the American MNC affiliates often must or do have contacts; or they are persons with whom such contacts do not exist but, perhaps, should. They are fundamentally the kinds of persons who, as suggested earlier, can and do greatly affect the present operations as well as the future course of U.S. business ventures in the countries involved.

A second structural factor we probed is the relationship between the parent company and its affiliates. We will suggest that this relationship represents a very thorny problem that deeply influences how U.S. companies are perceived and evaluated in Italy and Canada. The problem cannot be easily resolved by more or less sophisticated attempts to apply at the international level theories of complex organizations and their management that evolve in the United States.

A third structural factor involves the relationship between the U.S.-MNC and the Federal Government of the United States. As we will show later in this report, the policies of the Federal Government are a major factor in the actual overseas operations and evaluations of U.S. MNC's. But we were also interested in learning what kinds of contacts and communications are maintained between the executive or legislative branch of the Federal Government and the U.S. companies at home or overseas. Our findings will not be entirely encouraging, and will also require considerable further thought.

Choice of Countries

Canada and Italy are not ''typical'' countries, except in the very broad sense that they belong to the developed industrial as opposed to the less developed category of nations. In this first phase of the Conference Board's research activity on this general topic, we wished to begin with countries that might offer us special insights into the basic questions we are pursuing.

Canada is appealing on many counts. These include its special relationship to the United States, the proportion of U.S. overseas direct investment located there, the close interdependence of the two economies, and the Canadian restiveness about this interdependence. Canada also provided an unusual opportunity to probe elite attitudes that are typical of developed countries, and also, to a degree, of underdeveloped countries.

American investment in Italy is much smaller than in Canada. Nevertheless there are about 700 American firms operating in Italy, in a wide variety of activities and at markedly different levels of investment input. More important, however, is the possibility that Italy today may represent—along many dimensions and for better or for worse—exactly where other European countries will find themselves in a few years. We are thinking about patterns of welfare payments, industrial relations, cost of labor, relationships between trade unions and political parties, relative weight of the public sector in the national economy, and the like.

Italy is of considerable interest for two other reasons. First, like Canada, Italy has had one of the most liberal policies in the world regarding the conditions governing direct foreign investment there. This policy now seems destined to change quite substantially. Second, it is from Italy that there now emanates the leadership for something called the "Eurocommunism" movement. This movement has most direct implications for the future of MNC's not merely in Italy but elsewhere in Europe as well. Understanding Italy, we suggest, will provide a better basis for understanding probable Europeanwide developments and their implications.

Underlying Assumptions

We proceeded with this study on the basis of several assumptions. We assume that managers of private corporations have an inescapable responsibility to the "bottom line," but that they do *not* believe that this responsibility is always or even frequently at odds with the idea of good and responsible corporate citizenship.

We assume further that good corporate citizenship should not be thought of as meaning the same thing in all countries, or even that it will mean the same thing in a given country over time.

We also assume that the very nature of the multinational enterprise assures that there will be points of tension between it and the strategic elites of the host country. Extending overseas, however well-adapted the technologies, the managerial and marketing styles, the forms of organization evolved in the United States, is a delicate matter. The idea that it can happen without serious tensions from time to time is illusory. We assume, therefore, that understanding these points of tension is an essential first step toward making the MNC a viable and responsible enterprise overseas in the years ahead.

Our micro-level approach means that we will not pretend to provide answers to the cosmic questions people are debating about the MNC's. More often than not, those we have interviewed in this study will speak for themselves, either through paraphrase or direct quotation. What they have to say, we believe, may throw some light on the cosmic questions; more important, these observations may serve to modify in some modest way what it is that U.S. companies, at home or abroad, do or refrain from doing regarding their overseas operations.

Chapter 2
Canadian and Italian Settings

CANADA and Italy are recent nation-states, dating from the second half of the last century. As chronicled by Hugh Aitken, Canada's emergence as an independent nation within the British Empire was defensive; it was a response to the threat of absorption by the United States.[1] Italy's unification was aggressive; the House of Savoy, led by Cavour, managed to weave together a delicate national fabric, against the will of the organized Church, as well as many other local powerholders on the Peninsula.

Canadian leaders, as well as some of Italy's nation builders, understood that aspirations of national integration and independence were closely tied to the development of a vigorous national economy. And yet, in neither young country would economic development be able to proceed without considerable assistance of foreign capital.

Early Economic Development

In order to stimulate indigenous economic development, Canada developed the "National Policy" of high tariff walls. An unanticipated result of these barriers was to stimulate the formation in Canada of subsidiaries of foreign corporations. But as a matter of actual practice, despite the objectives of the "National Policy," Canada has traditionally been extremely liberal in encouraging the inflow of capital from outside the country. Not until the late 1950's, in fact, were significant restrictions on foreign investment even considered by the Canadian Government.

Following Italian unification, the northern state of Piedmont imposed its own tariff system throughout the new nation. In many cases this had the effect of lowering previously existing regional tariffs that were designed to protect nascent industry, and considerable overall disequilibrium followed. For this and other reasons industrial development in Italy was quite late, lagging at least fifty years behind that of Great Britain.

Canadian economic development was also slow, owing in considerable measure to its small population, which in 1900 numbered only 5.4 million, and to the great size of the country. In both countries the take-off toward industrial development occurred in the years preceding World War I; it is only after World War II, however, that both countries became modern industrial states. In both, the achievement of this transformation involved a very heavy dependence on foreign capital.

Foreign capital had also been present in the initial economic evolution of these countries. In the early years of Canadian confederation, outside financing was

---

[1] Hugh G. J. Aitken, "The Changing Structure of the Canadian Economy," in H. G. J. Aitken *et al.*, *The American Economic Impact on Canada,* Durham, N.C.: Duke University Commonwealth Studies Center, 1959, pp. 3-4.

used to construct railways, canals, roads and other public utilities, to develop Canada's natural resources, and to initiate manufacturing industries. The "Gray Report" observes that prior to World War I foreign capital played a greater role in Canadian economic development than any time before or since, and thus in relative terms this was the time when such inputs had their greatest impact on the Canadian economy.[2] Most of this early investment was not direct but of the portfolio variety, and until World War I most of it was provided by Britain in the form of debt securities from the London bond market.

Although it proceeded at a snail's pace, Italy's economic development also drew upon foreign capital. One striking characteristic of Italy's industrialization was the direct involvement of the public sector. In effect, the political leaders of Piedmont exchanged high tariffs on certain agricultural products with the large landowners of the South for a free hand in the use of public, private and foreign capital to bring about the geographic industrial concentration that continues to exist north of Rome. The Industrial Triangle—bounded by Milan, Turin and Genoa—which remains the country's most important creator of gross national product, has in recent years continued to attract disproportionate shares of the indigenous and foreign capital invested in Italy's further development.

Between the two major wars of this century the rate of increase of foreign capital was quite low in both countries. Total foreign investment in Canada doubled between 1900 and 1914, doubled again between 1914 and 1930, and fell off somewhat during the Great Depression. But during this period two important changes occurred in the character of foreign investment there. First, the United States replaced Britain as the primary source of such capital; U.S. capital accounted for three-fifths of the total by 1930. Second, there gradually occurred a shift from portfolio to direct investment, as U.S. investors displayed a preference for this form.

In Italy inputs of foreign investment were abruptly reduced with the advent of Fascism and its policies of economic autarchy. Mussolini's efforts to make Italy economically self-sufficient fell afoul of many problems, including the Depression. As Italian industries, in which Italian banks had tied up too much capital, began to fail, so did the banks. The Fascist government's solution was to create the Institute for Industrial Reconstruction to buy up from the banks the equities of these failing companies. This step accelerated a historical trend of public intervention that has made Italian industry today the most "socialized" in Western Europe. This massive presence of government enterprise in the industrial sector remains a basic fact that conditions the present and future use of foreign capital in that country.

Development after World War II

Direct American investment in Canada and Italy expanded rapidly after 1945. At war's end great numbers of U.S. firms established subsidiaries and branches in

[2] *Foreign Direct Investment in Canada*. Ottawa: Government of Canada, 1972, pp. 13-15. This report was drafted under the direction of the Honorable Herbert E. Gray, P.C., M.P., then Minister of National Revenue in the Canadian Government.

Canada in order to gain access to a rapidly expanding market which was protected by tariffs on a wide range of manufactured products. Entering the Canadian market was also a means of gaining access to the markets of the British Commonwealth.

During this period, American direct investment in manufacturing, mining and petroleum increased substantially. At the same time, the share of Canadian industry controlled by foreign—and especially U.S. —firms grew significantly. Both of these developments are summarized in Tables 2-1 and 2-2 .

Italy's postwar situation was also attractive to American investors. Classical attractions such as lower labor costs were present there, as was somewhat later the tariff wall against outsiders erected by the European Communities. Beyond these factors was a market and demand structure that was expanding more rapidly in Italy in the 1950's than in the United States. So American firms entered Italy in order to gain stable control of a share of expanding markets, to meet their international competition in this market, and to expand the overall context in which U.S. industry could exploit the advantages created by America's superiority in research and development.

American direct investment in Italy was also greatly spurred by the Vanoni Law (No. 43) of 1956, which created unusually liberal conditions regarding such investments. The Italians then guaranteed unhampered repatriation of capital and earnings, made no discrimination at all between national and foreign companies, and on many kinds of investment, defined as "productive," there were no currency exchange restrictions. In 1958, the Italians passed additional legislation that made it possible to export and import freely, at the official exchange rate, any amount of capital registered in a variety of "capital accounts." This system prevailed until 1973. The fact that it encouraged considerable inflow of investment from abroad is widely recognized, and attested to by the data reported in Table 2-3.

Note that Table 2-3 summarizes only those investment projects that qualified as "productive"; the total inflow of capital from abroad was much greater. Bank of

Table 2-1: Direct Foreign Investments in Canada (book value in billions of dollars)

	Total		Manufacturing		Petroleum		Mining and Smelting	
	Total	U.S.	Total	U.S.	Total	U.S.	Total	U.S.
1930	$2.4	$2.0	$1.5	$1.2	$0.2	$0.1	$0.3	$0.2
1939	2.3	1.9	1.4	1.2	n.a.	n.a.	0.3	0.3
1946	2.8	2.4	1.9	1.6	0.2	0.2	0.4	0.3
					(1945)	(1945)		
1950	4.0	3.4	2.8	2.3	0.7	0.7	0.6	0.5
					(1951)	(1951)		
1954	6.8	5.8	3.9	3.1	1.5	1.4	1.1	0.9
1960	12.9	10.5	6.5	5.1	3.7	3.2	2.0	1.7
1967	20.7	17.0	10.6	9.0	6.0	4.9	3.4	2.9

Source: John Fayerweather, *Foreign Investment in Canada*. White Plains, New York: International Arts and Sciences Press, Inc., 1973, p. 6.

Table 2-2: Foreign Control as a Percentage of Selected Canadian Industries, Selected Year-ends, 1926-1967

Industry	1926	1939	1948	1956	1960	1963	1967
Percentage of total control by all nonresidents							
Manufacturing	35	38	43	52	59	60	59
Petroleum and natural gas				80	73	74	74
Mining and smelting	38	42	40	58	61	59	65
Railways	3	3	3	2	2	2	2
Other utilities	20	26	24	6	5	4	5
Totals of above industries	17	21	25	31	33	34	35
and merchandising							
Percentage of total control by U.S. residents							
Manufacturing	30	32	39	41	44	46	n.a.
Petroleum and natural gas				73	64	62	n.a.
Mining and smelting	32	38	37	52	53	52	n.a.
Railways	3	3	3	2	2	2	n.a.
Other utilities	20	26	24	4	4	4	n.a.
Totals of above industries	15	19	22	26	26	27	28
and merchandising							

Source: 1926-1963: Isaiah A. Litvak and Christopher J. Maule, eds., *Foreign Investment: The Experience of Host Countries*. New York: Praeger, 1970, p. 86

1967: Grant Reuber, "Foreign Investment in Canada: A Review," in D. A. L. Auld, ed., *Economics: Contemporary Issues in Canada*. Toronto: Holt, Rinehart, & Winston, 1972, p. 164.

Italy data, for example, which do not agree with other data sources (see Table 2-4) place the level of foreign investment for selected postwar years at the following levels:

Year	Amount (in $ millions)
1961	$ 334
1964	900
1966	579
1968	660
1970	1,161
1971	1,219
1973	1,142
1974	1,281

Statistics on the amounts of American direct overseas investment differ, depending on the source from which the statistics are drawn. United States Department of Commerce estimates for 1973 were $2.3 billion in Italy compared with $28 billion of U.S. direct investment in Canada. Summary information for Italy, Europe and Canada is provided in Table 2-4. It is worth remarking that between 1960 and the early 1970's, American direct investments in Italy, which had still been at a relatively low level in 1950, increased by more than seven times, while the increase in Canada was only two-and-a-half times.

Table 2-3: Foreign Direct Investment in Italy Under Law 43 of 1956

Description	1972	Total 1956-72
	(in millions of dollars)	
Total registered investment*	$31.4	$1,215.9
Breakdown by industry		
Petroleum	—	477.4
Chemical or pharmaceutical	3.1	182.0
Metal working	2.2	86.7
Engineering	2.9	123.7
Food	0.4	60.4
Hotel and tourism	0.9	30.3
All other	21.9	255.4
Breakdown by region		
Northern Italy	24.6	842.8
Southern Italy	6.7	373.1
Breakdown by country of investor		
United States	19.3	507.4
United Kingdom	1.9	198.0
Switzerland	5.2	182.0
Germany	—	139.3
France	2.8	64.7
All other countries	2.2	124.5

Source: Banca Nazionale del Lavoro, *Italian Trends,* Vol. 8, August, 1973.

* Amount of foreign exchange transfers at (then) current prices (converted into dollars at the Smithsonian central rate).

Several surveys conducted in Italy beginning in the mid-1960's suggest that approximately one-fifth of total industrial investment in that country is accounted for by direct foreign capital inputs. The American share of this seems to have declined from well over 40 percent earlier to about 25 percent in more recent years.[3] However, as one would imagine, the relative importance of U.S. investments varies considerably by industrial sector. Information drawn from a variety of sources suggests that in the 1970's the United States' share of various Italian markets looks something like what is depicted by Table 2-5.

One may want to add to this information the research finding that whereas in the early 1960's the number of foreign-owned firms among the largest 194 Italian enterprises was 46, accounting for 17 percent of total sales, in 1971 the number of foreign-owned firms in this group of 194 had increased to 60, with the proportion of total sales reaching 26 percent.[4]

Developments such as these lead increasing numbers of Italians to express concern about the growing dependence of Italian industry on outside ownership. But the Italian situation is relatively less intense by comparison with Canada's. As

[3] Banca Nazionale del Lavoro, *Italian Trends,* Vol. 8, August, 1973.
[4] G. L. Alzona, "Crisi della grandi concentrazioni industriali," *L'Impresa,* November-December, 1972, p. 419.

Table 2-4: U.S. Direct Foreign Investment (millions of dollars, end of year)

	1950	1960	1970	1973 (preliminary)
Developed Countries	$ 5,679	$19,328	$53,145	$ 74,084
Canada	3,579	11,198	22,790	28,055
Europe..........................	1,733	6,681	24,516	37,218
Italy	63	384	1,550	2,301
Developing Countries	5,735	12,032	21,448	27,867
All Areas	11,788	32,778	78,178	107,268

Sources: U.S. Department of Commerce, *Survey of Current Business*, August 1962, November 1972, August 1974.

Table 2-5: Shares of Various Markets Going to U.S. Firms Operating in Italy (circa 1970-71)

Industry	Percentage Market Share
Chemicals	8.3%
Chemical (including cosmetics .... and petrochemicals)	20.0
Retail	13.5
Electromechanical (including .... computers)	28.0
Pharmaceuticals	35.8
Petroleum	33.9

Sources: J. J. Bodewyn and D. C. Grosser, "American Direct Investments in Italy," *Review of the Economic Conditions of Italy*, Vol. 26, September, 1972, p. 363; CESPE, "La presenza in Italia di società multinazionali stranieri," *Politica ed economia*, 1971, N. 2-3, pp. 35-41.

can be seen in Table 2-2 above, some 35 percent of Canadian manufacturing industry was under foreign control as early as 1926. By 1960, this figure had grown to 59 percent, of which 44 percent was controlled by U.S. residents. Almost three-quarters of Canada's petroleum and natural gas industry and two-thirds of its mining and smelting industries were foreign-controlled at this time. Of Canada's 100 largest firms, 39 were controlled by foreign companies in 1966, 26 of which were U.S.-based.[5]

Second Thoughts

In both Canada and Italy, earlier relaxed economic relationships are now more tense, concurrent with the growth registered by U.S. industrial and related ven-

[5] Isaiah A. Litvak and Christopher J. Maule, "Foreign Investment in Canada," in Isaiah A. Litvak and Christopher J. Maule, eds., *Foreign Investment: The Experience of Host Countries*. New York: Praeger, 1970, p. 88.

tures in both countries. Today there are in excess of 4,000 affiliates of U.S. firms in Canada, and about 700 in Italy. Tensions are to be expected when transformations of local ownership reach such proportions in a very short time.

Canada and the "Special Relationship"

In the Canadian case the common U.S.-Canadian effort during World War II led to economic ties that were strengthened following war's end. The United States had in fact become Canada's major supplier of imports before it became Canada's primary source of capital. During the war, the United States became Canada's largest export market as well. By the mid-1950's, with 60 percent of Canadian exports going to the United States and 70 percent of Canadian imports coming from across the border, the two countries had become each other's major trading partner.

This mutually beneficial interaction was seen as one dimension of the "special relationship" that linked the two countries. For at least a generation following the war, it was to symbolize a close and cooperative relationship. "Most of the people on both sides of the border thought of the bilateral relationship as a 'continental,' North American partnership, involving both an increased degree of mutually beneficial economic integration and the close coordination of defense and political policies with regard to the rest of the world." [6]

In the late 1950's Canadians began to question the attractiveness of the special relationship. The Canadian economist, Hugh G. J. Aitken warned of Canada's increasing economic dependence on the United States. He expressed concern that it ill behooved Canada to lessen her dependence on the rest of the world while at the same time becoming more dependent on her neighbor to the south. In 1958, too, the Royal Commission on Canada's Economic Prospects officially posed the question of foreign ownership as an issue requiring government policy decisions and intervention.[7]

By 1961 opinion polls were showing that a majority of Canadians now felt that there was "enough U.S. capital in Canada now." Within ten years the number of Canadians willing to express the idea of "enough" had increased to over two-thirds. Although Canadians continued to agree that the U.S. role in their country's economic development had been a good thing, this did not keep them from adding that in more recent times the U.S. ownership of Canadian companies might have a bad effect on the country.

Research conducted by the Business Studies Research Unit of the University of Windsor showed that between 1969 and 1973 the number of Canadians who thought the American investment there was a "good thing" fell from 51 percent to 32 percent, while those who said it was a "bad thing" increased from 34 percent to 43 percent. Even the poorer provinces, which might be expected to be much more

---

[6] John M. Volpe, "Canadian-American Economic Relations; Sources and Resolution of Conflicts," *The Canadian Business Review,* Summer, 1974, p. 35.

[7] Aitken, *op. cit.,* p. 9; *Royal Commission on Canada's Economic Prospects, Final Report.* Ottawa: The Queen's Printer, 1958.

favorable to foreign investment capital, showed attitudes moving in this direction.[8] John Sloan Dickey, who has studied Canadian-American relations for many years, puts the matter this way:

"The division of views that exists in Canada today about the American presence is not over whether or not it is a major factor in Canadian life but rather over how serious it is as a threat and how it should be met. The main disagreement is whether some of the proposed remedies, particularly in the control of foreign investment, would not be more harmful to Canada and individual Canadians than an often irksome ubiquitous American presence." [9]

Italy and the "Economic Miracle"

It is apparent that similar transformations in public opinion are at work in Italy. As long as the country continued to experience the "economic miracle" that began in the late 1950's and carried well into the 1960's, relatively little attention was paid to the presence of foreign investors in the nation's economy. Indeed, public opinion data show that Italians, more than most other West Europeans, welcomed foreign, particularly American, capital, and felt overwhelmingly that it brought important benefits to the country. The views of the public tended to echo those of the elites. Both provided a strong basis of support for the unusually liberal governmental policies toward foreign investments maintained by the Italian government throughout the postwar period.

As economic conditions began to deteriorate, so did support for liberal policies toward foreign investors. Attitudes toward multinationals, particularly American MNC's, were eroded by a number of dramatic episodes involving the abandonment of Italy by firms (European as well as American) that employed several hundred (and sometimes several thousand) persons. Although these decisions to disinvest involve multinationals from other European countries as well, and although the disinvestment decisions represent a small fraction of the MNC's operating in Italy, widespread media coverage and trade union protests serve to greatly multiply their public impact.

In addition, recent revelations regarding the political contributions of some MNC's in Italy, and the alleged secret payments made by American corporations to high government officials, help to bring about a radical change in public images of and attitudes toward the foreign investor. Except for one or two important industrial sectors to be explored later, it is fair to say that Italians do not share the Canadian fear, often obsessively articulated, of dependence on the United States.

[8] See John H. Sigler and Dennis Goresky, "Public Opinion on United States-Canadian Relations," *International Organization,* Autumn, 1974, pp. 648-9, 645; J. Alex Murray, "Canadian Public Attitudes Toward Foreign Equity Investment and Economic Policy," *Hearings* Before the Joint Economic Committee of the 94th Congress of the United States (1975), "Tables and Charts," p. 4; and John Fayerweather, *Foreign Investment in Canada.* White Plains, New York: International Arts and Sciences Press, Inc., 1973, Chapter 2.

[9] John Sloan Dickey, "Canada Independent," *Foreign Affairs,* July, 1972, p. 688.

Nevertheless, the modified views toward foreign investment, particularly as they are held and expressed by Italians with political clout, warrant careful attention and appraisal.

Nationalism and Other Noneconomic Issues

It would be a mistake to associate the rising trends of public opinion hostile to an American economic presence simply with the increasing control of local industry by U.S. investors. In 1948, for example, foreign firms controlled about 43 percent of Canadian manufacturing, but Canadians then expressed little concern about this; indeed, the Canadian government was at that time actually encouraging an even greater capital inflow. Even in the 1960's, when foreign control of Canadian manufacturing peaked at about 60 percent, there were many Canadians who felt that this was desirable and actually reflected the strength and the attractiveness of the Canadian economy.

In fact, by this time the American investor had begun to turn away from Canada and to direct attention to the rapidly expanding European economies such as Italy's. Thus, by 1970 Canada's share of U.S. foreign direct investment had declined from 34 percent (1960) to 29 percent; and by 1973 it had fallen to 26 percent. In absolute terms, of course, U.S. investment in Canada continued to increase at least until 1973. During this same period (1960-1973) American direct investments in Western Europe increased sixfold; by the mid-1960's, 19 percent of U.S.-MNC affiliates were located in Canada, but 37 percent of them were found in Western Europe.[10]

In both Canada and Italy a wide variety of factors—both political and economic—go into explaining a certain growing disenchantment with the American firm. In the 1960's Canada began to experience the kind of nationalism that would inevitably call into question the costs and benefits of massive American and other foreign economic presence in the country. Nationalists like Kari Levitt argued that Canada's economic development benefited the owners of foreign capital more than Canadians, and that these investments somehow perpetuated Canada's status vis-à-vis other countries, but particularly the United States, as a "hewer of wood and drawer of water." Indeed Levitt claimed that "Present-day Canada may be described as the world's richest underdeveloped country." [11]

In Italy it could be claimed that the fifty percent drop in the value of Italian common stock between 1961 and 1972 provoked a large-scale take-over of Italian companies by foreigners. It is a striking fact that, whereas earlier American direct investments in Italy involved the creation of new productive enterprises, that situation shifted quite dramatically to take-overs in the late 1960's. In any event, echos of Canadian complaints are found in Luigi Preti's cynical remark that Italy

[10] See above Table 2-1 and United Nations, *Multinational Corporations in World Development,* ST/ECA/190, p. 143.

[11] Kari Levitt, *Silent Surrender; the Multinational Corporation in Canada.* Toronto: Macmillan of Canada, 1970, p. 25.

was becoming "a colonial republic founded on our work for the profit of others." [12]

Relations between Canadians and Italians, on the one hand, and the United States, on the other, were also strained by such things as U.S. foreign policy, especially in Southeast Asia, the devaluation of the American dollar, trade issues, restrictions on Canadian imports, the extraterritorial application of United States laws to U.S. affiliate firms operating in Italy and Canada, defense issues such as NATO, and U.S. control over nuclear weapons in Canada. The situation in Italy, of course, was greatly aggravated by the political radicalization that occurred in the late 1960's, by growing evidence that the country's traditional governmental forces could no longer govern the country or guide the economy with any degree of stability or predictability, and by the prospect that the Italian Communist Party might come to play a much more significant political role, not only in Italy but in Western Europe.

Issues involving the American presence in the national economy are much more politicized in Canada than in Italy. In 1958, the first of several official Canadian reports on the subject was published. This was followed by the *Report on Foreign Ownership and the Structure of Canadian Industry* (1968), the report on *Foreign Direct Investment in Canada* (1972), and the *Report of the Ontario Select Committee on Economic and Cultural Nationalism* (1975). Substantial investigations on these topics were also undertaken by the Science Council of Canada, the Economic Council of Canada, and the Economic Council of Ontario; a variety of reports and statements were made public.

By 1966, the three major federal political parties had more or less well-developed positions on these matters. On the whole the electoral impact of the more narrowly focused issue of U.S. ownership of Canadian industry still seemed low in the early 1970's. But the more general issue of Canada's cultural, economic and political autonomy vis-à-vis the United States increasingly colored the political environment. New policy initiatives were designed to enhance Canadian independence and yet to minimize the danger of political and economic isolation.

In neither the Canadian nor the Italian case should evidence of nationalism be confused with impulses to retreat and to become isolated within their own borders. As the Canadian-American Committee noted not too long ago: "Canadian nationalism is not expressed solely as a movement away from internationalism into purely domestic concerns and solutions but, in fact, often seeks further overseas contacts as an alternative to what it perceives to be the threat of 'continentalism.' "[13]

Indeed, as of June 1976, Canada is associated with the European Communities in a special economic and commercial pact. Italy, too, is exploring new sets of

---

[12] L. Preti, *Italia Malata*. Milan: Mursia, 1973, p. 121, cited in K. Allen and A. Stevenson, *An Introduction to the Italian Economy*. New York: Harper and Row, 1975, p. 44. The wording is a play on the opening words of the Italian Constitution.

[13] *The New Environment for Canadian-American Relations, A Statement by the Canadian-American Committee*. Washington, D. C.: National Planning Association, 1972, p. 26.

international economic relationships, some of them within the context of the European Communities, others in stepped-up contacts and relationships with countries like Japan and Canada. Neither wants to be entrapped by overdependence on the United States, although neither is prepared to terminate, nor perhaps even seriously to transform, that relationship.

This is also part of the changing environment confronting American multinationals. We can now turn to a detailed exploration of the Canadian and Italian environments at close-range.

Part Two
MNC's and National Development

Chapter 3
The Problem of Dependency

Elites in Italy and Canada widely acknowledge the contributions of U.S. MNC's to domestic economic growth and industrial development. Respondents note that MNC's have been vital agents of modernization: Mobilizing capital, spreading technology, developing indigenous managerial skills, and, in many cases, opening access to overseas markets. Foreign capital enabled a relatively small population of Canadians to develop a vast country and to maintain standards of living on a par with her southern neighbor. In Italy, as in Western Europe in general, U.S. investments and MNC's provided support for rapid rates of economic growth after World War II. The percentage of annual increase in MNC sales still greatly exceeds growth rates of gross national product there. In both countries the salutary role of the MNC is unquestioned, except by those few groups whose real target is more likely to be the capitalist system of production than MNC's in particular.

A Case of Ambivalence

Elites in both countries with whom we spoke also agree that future prospects for economic growth are dependent to a high degree on the continued participation of MNC's in the national economies. Although U.S. MNC's have been the object of much criticism in recent years in Italy and, for a rather longer period, in Canada, not a single person interviewed says that his country would be better off in the future without the presence of U.S. MNC's. Italian government and party elites, including—and perhaps especially—the leaders of the Left, emphasize Italy's need for the continued cooperation and inputs of U.S. MNC's. As one Communist leader observed:

"I will say that a modern economy like Italy's will simply have to accept the presence of multinationals here. . . . One must predict that they will be present in a mixed economy and in an economy where there must be considerable cooperation not only between small and large corporations, but also between the public and private sectors."

In any future evolution of the Italian economy, "There is no question at all that multinationals will be present."

In Canada, where pressures on U.S. MNC's deriving from governmental policy have been substantially greater (and where even more pressure is threatened), there is widespread concern among elites that Canadian attempts to squeeze MNC's for more benefits to Canada will wind up mortally injuring the geese that lay the golden eggs. A senior adviser to the Canadian government, who had helped develop Canada's recent legislation on foreign investment, takes pains to note that these policies in no way reverse Canada's traditional openness to external investment. Others observe that, when all is said and done, "Canada still remains the most hospitable place for U.S. investment." In terms of the questions posed by this study, the elites we interviewed provide an unequivocal basic reply: They recognize past contributions of U.S. MNC's and the continuing presence of these firms is considered highly desirable.

In Italy, an official of the General Confederation of Italian Industry documents the reasons for considering MNC's desirable. He points to a study conducted by his organization involving the comparative analysis of a sample of Italian and foreign-owned firms.[1] That study shows, he says, that foreign-owned firms, and particularly U.S. firms, outperform local firms in a number of areas. They also tend to have a valuable stabilizing effect on the economy. Among the findings he cites from that study are:

(1) In situations involving economic downturn, foreign-owned firms are less inclined than local firms to contract investments.

(2) Sales per employee are much higher in foreign-owned firms. In addition, rates of growth in the gross products of these firms far outpace annual increments in GNP.

(3) Although cost of labor is higher in foreign-owned firms, this factor is somewhat balanced by higher productivity, greater capacity to reinvest, greater financial flexibility and staying power.

In effect this official, like many others we interviewed, believes that beyond whatever contributions the multinationals make in the development of products and markets, or the opening up of new sectors for investment, the demonstration effect of how they operate as enterprises is of great value to Italy.

There are, of course, many responsible critics of U.S. MNC's in each country. They consider it desirable that U.S. policy makers in the Federal Government and parent MNC's should pay close attention to what they say. They express the hope that U.S. MNC's will continue to play significant—and profitable—roles in their countries. They add that the rules and expectations that have guided the behavior and operations of MNC's in the past are now changing. The critical issue for U.S. MNC's, therefore, is not whether they are wanted in the future, but whether they can adapt to these new rules; whether they can accommodate to new ways of distributing the costs and benefits of their activities abroad.

Canadian and Italian respondents agree that U.S. firms came into their countries at particularly advantageous moments. The local situations were much in their favor; there were overwhelming needs for capital, employment and technical and managerial know-how. They believe that U.S. MNC's played a vital role in developing and modernizing their countries. But they add that MNC's made

---

[1] See Confederazione Generale dell'Industria Italiana, *Indagine su un gruppo di imprese industriali a partecipazione estera*. Rome: Editore SIPI, 1974. This study leaves something to be desired on the methodological side, as the authors themselves acknowledge. It deals with a sample of 295 firms, for only 151 of which data permitting quantitative analysis were available. In any case, the authors are careful to spell out how, and on the basis of what criteria, the analyzed companies differ.

substantial profits, too. The benefits were mutual; the slate is clean; and no one owes the multinationals anything. Now that needs have lessened, U.S. firms seeking to carry on business abroad will have to worry about other matters—more about what host countries want out of the relationship; more about how MNC's can make themselves more acceptable corporate citizens.

Canadian views of U.S. MNC's are easier to describe; Canadians have been consciously worrying, talking and writing about the topic for a longer time. In the first place, many of the issues involving U.S. MNC's in Canada are seen as a dimension of the wider question of the future of Canadian-U.S. relations. Canadians are more concerned about the political and cultural impact of Canada's economic ties with the United States than about the economic ties themselves. They feel that the depth of Canadian concerns about national identity and independence—what many Canadians with whom we spoke called "pro-Canadianism"—is not well understood, either in Washington, or among U.S. firms with subsidiaries in Canada. Canadians, and also Americans in Canada, lament the lack of knowledge of Canada in the United States. A former U.S. Foreign Service officer and expert on Canada observes that "the level of ignorance about Canada among U.S. businessmen is about as high as the level of trade between the United States and Canada."

Italy is not like this. As we saw in Chapter 2, the Italian economy is not as dominated by American firms as is Canada's. Italy does not share a border with the United States; nor is it viewed by Americans or Italians as the "51st state." Distance and language alone ensure that managers of U.S. firms operating in Italy will be aware of the "foreignness" of the place. Some Italian elites even believe this is carried too far. They would prefer, for example, that American managers speak more Italian and become more integrated into the Italian community.

Thus, though Italy has of late experienced waves of anti-Americanism, the surge of nationalism that has occurred in Canada in the past ten or fifteen years is absent there. Furthermore, Italian attacks on multinationals are of very recent vintage, stemming *not* from obsessive feelings of dependency on the United States but, rather, from the shock and the aftermath of serious national economic crises.

The Question of Canadian Identity

Canadians are greatly concerned that the long-term impact of Canadian-U.S. relations may fatally weaken Canada's national identity. This is a base line that conditions their attitudes toward U.S. firms. Italians are not really concerned about national identity. By and large they believe that the nation-state can cope reasonably well with the multinationals. Where the problems—real or imagined—created by the latter seem intractable, Italians are ready to reach for Europeanwide instrumentalities to cope with them.

The 1972 report on *Foreign Direct Investment in Canada* (the Gray Report) summarizes earlier Canadian surveys on this issue and provides the core of Canada's—especially Ottawa's—conventional wisdom of the impact of MNC's. The report underscores possible imbalance between the manufacturing and resource sector that might be created or exacerbated by multinational activity. It stresses, too, the tendency of U.S. subsidiaries in Canada to replicate the full range of products produced by the parent firm, at significantly lower profit levels in the smaller Canadian market. Beyond this, the report scores the incidence of "truncated firms," which do not perform all of the essential tasks associated with the development, production and marketing of products in Canada and abroad.[2]

Few of the Canadians we interviewed feel that MNC's are in themselves the *cause* of these problems. Most suggest that Canadian economic policies in the past—tax, tariff and competition policies in particular—are largely responsible for the present domination of Canada's economy by U.S. firms. Many argue that it was Canada's determination to catch up with U.S. standards of living that led Canadian leaders to encourage external investment on such a massive scale. They believe it is now necessary for Canada to modify policies that encourage too many U.S. firms to establish subsidiaries or branch plants there. In the future, they say, it must be shown that foreign-owned firms will provide considerable benefit for Canada.

Canadians rarely take a one-sided view of the basic problem. Nevertheless even those opposed to the strong nationalist view agree that the weight of U.S. capital in the country is preoccupying. Thus, the head of a major research organization that opposes the nationalist view says: "There is no denying that there is a large, powerful and probably excessive presence of U.S. firms in Canada." He, like most others, wants to search for that mix of policies that would simultaneously increase Canadian benefits from foreign investment, develop greater indigenous scientific, developmental, managerial and entrepreneurial skills, and increase the ratio of Canadian to foreign ownership in the economy.

Italy's Multifaceted Problems

In Italy there is much less concern expressed about the impact of foreign investment on the economy. Indeed, Italians these days are much more preoccupied with the possibility that the weight of foreign investment may diminish, as American and European firms find it more attractive to invest elsewhere.

Nevertheless, as many of our respondents point out, there has been marked increase of attention to MNC's, and they have come under considerable attack. Cases of attempted or successful multinational disinvestment, revelations regarding political contributions and corruption, the energy crisis, growing controversy over the construction of nuclear power stations—these and other events have made the issue of the multinationals much more salient.

Italian criticism of multinationals is much more diverse. To be sure, there are some in Italy who, like some in Canada, view MNC's as "instruments of American imperialism" and expressions of "American monopoly capitalism." Communist party leaders, who assure us that their attitudes toward foreign capital are essentially open and neutral, insist on thinking, talking and writing about the MNC's in this vein. Nevertheless, they agree with many others all over the world

---

[2] *Foreign Direct Investment in Canada*. Ottawa: Government of Canada, 1972, pp. 5-8.

who argue how absurd it would be to try to suppress or deny the objective historical conditions that brought MNC's into existence in the first place.[3]

Bureaucrats and many political leaders in Italy are worried that multinationals, particularly those of the United States, have come to dominate sectors like energy and electronics that are considered vital to national development. Economists worry a lot about the possible snowballing effect of disinvestment, while intellectuals tend to focus on political pressures and corruption. Communists and trade unionists lean toward the view that the nation-state, at least the nation-state of Italy, is not completely able to control a wide variety of MNC activities; and so they promote the "Eurostrategy" discussed later.

It may be helpful to depict here the kinds of specific criticisms of multinationals that were *spontaneously* mentioned by the Italian elites interviewed (see Table 3-1). On the whole these were the kinds of criticism Italians supplied in their answers to the following question, asked early in the interview: "In general, what would you say are the major good points and bad points about American multinationals operating in this country?"

It should be noted that the first criticism is not against MNC's as such but against the Italian government because of its lack of a clear, coherent and rational policy regarding them.

Criticisms about take-overs, equity sharing, bureaucratization, tax evasion, labor relations, and so on were spontaneously mentioned less than three times. Furthermore all of the above and other criticisms were discussed, at times in considerable detail, in response to specific probing questions. For example, Italians who talked about centralization of decisions at the center, or about the "long hand" of the United States in answer to the question, "How would you describe the relationship between the parent and its affiliate?" are not included in the above frequency count.

Among all of the Italian elites interviewed only three—a Socialist journalist and intellectual, a Christian Democratic bureaucrat, and a former cabinet minister— claimed they knew little or nothing about American MNC's. This turned out to be only partly the case with the first two, and not the case at all with the third. But all of them had quite strong impressions and opinions about the multinationals. A senior bureaucrat sees this as being in striking contrast to earlier times, when the MNC's were largely ignored. In the context of Italy's unusually liberal policies toward foreign investment, and the well-being produced by Italy's "economic miracle," the bureaucrat notes that attitudes "were quite benign, if not absolutely favorable." He adds:

"There was a great deal of legislation and administrative regulation in the past that facilitated American investment in the country, and under the kind of long-range hegemony that the Christian Democrats have maintained, doing business in Italy was essentially a piece of cake for the American multinational corporation."

---

[3] For a basic statement on the MNC's coming from one of the Italian Communist party's leading economic analysts, see Eugenio Peggio, "Le società multinazionali e la sinistra europea," *Politica ed economia* Nos. 2/3, 1971, pp. 23-24.

Table 3-1: Spontaneous Criticisms of Multinationals

Type of Criticism: "Bad Points"	Number of Mentions
Italy's lack of policy on MNC's	22
Disinvestment and abandonment	17
U.S. domination of vital sectors	10
Lack of local research and development	10
Financial, monetary maneuvers	9
Extraterritoriality of U.S. laws	9
MNC's not really multinational	8
Inability of Italy to control	7
Failure of MNC's to adapt	7
Rip-off investments	6
Conflict with national goals	4
Information disclosure	3
MNC's lack credibility	3

Although Italians acknowledge that the laws on foreign investment of 1956 and later do constitute a de facto national policy, they believe the policy is entirely antiquated and requires considerable updating. The probable content of such a new policy is discussed later in this report.

Regionalism: A Different Problem from Nationalism

In the early 1970's, it was useful to draw distinctions in Canada between "radical nationalists," "strong nationalists," and "moderate nationalists." It is questionable whether a similar analysis is useful today. The fringe of radical nationalists seems substantially weaker; the termination of the Vietnam War brought a diminution of anti-U.S. feeling. Vestiges of the various radical groups have coalesced; they oppose not only U.S. MNC's, but business and bigness in general.

At the same time, "moderate nationalism" has become more pervasive than ever before and most Canadians with whom we spoke see great value in the development of Canada's distinct and separate identity. So, along with less radical opposition to U.S. MNC's, there also exists wide support for the "screening process" for foreign investment which was established a few years ago. Thus, the chief executive officer of a major Canadian-owned company says he strongly opposes the nationalist viewpoint on MNC's, but observes that: "There has been substantial consensus in Canada on the need to monitor transactions, such as the acquisitions of foreign firms, on an individual basis, to ensure that the Canadian national interest is brought into the dealings."

Canadian senior executives included in our study strongly support the principle of review. Several of them—from both U.S. and Canadian firms there—observe that although they were initially not in favor of the process they have "come to realize that similar screening and review processes had been carried on in Mexico, Japan and elsewhere with little detrimental effect on foreign investment."

Canada: Federal-Provincial Tensions

Regional differences in perceptions of the impact of foreign investment and MNC's in Canada are extremely important. The development of policy by the federal government has been made much more complex and difficult by the fact that under the Canadian constitution many critical areas of current attention, such as economic growth, employment and, perhaps most importantly, resource development fall under provincial jurisdiction. The growth of federal-provincial tensions around these issues has often involved foreign firms in difficult "no-win" cross-pressures.

National opinion surveys show that provincial differences on attitudes toward foreign investment have diminished sharply in recent years, but our interviews reveal that elite differences remain substantial. In the first place, in the less affluent—mainly eastern—provinces fear is expressed that current federal policies will lead to a declining inflow of foreign capital, and thus jeopardize still further the shaky economies of the relatively less-developed parts of the nation.

Governments of several provinces have mounted extensive campaigns to attract new foreign investment. These longer term differences between the more and less economically developed and industrialized provinces have been heightened in recent years by the sharp increase in regionalist sentiment throughout Canada. If richer western provinces and poorer eastern ones tend to disagree on the desirability and drawbacks of foreign direct investment, they are also increasingly of the view that "independence" from central Canada—from the financial and economic control of Toronto and the political control of Ottawa—is much to be desired.

An official of one of the Maritime provinces tells us: "We tend to see American economic imperialism as somewhat more benign than central Canadian imperialism. Economic nationalism," he continues, "is just one more gimmick to impose Toronto-Ottawa policies on the provinces." The publisher of a major newspaper in western Canada notes that as the sense of distinctiveness increased vis-à-vis the United States, it was accompanied by an increasing distinction between western and central Canada. "We are 3,000 miles from Ottawa," he says, "and Ottawa is 300,000 miles from us."

In western Canada, opposition to U.S. MNC's tends to focus on the exploitation of nonrenewable natural resources. As the western provinces become more affluent and, in certain areas such as British Columbia and Alberta, enjoy extraordinarily rapid rates of economic growth, they also become increasingly determined to assert control over indigenous mineral and energy resources. For them it is immaterial whether this means battling "foreign" owners in New York *or* Toronto.

Western Canadians, says another journalist in the area, "refused to continue to be the mere suppliers of raw materials for either the United States or central Canada." Recent clashes between U.S. MNC's and Canada over potash or oil, for example, have been seriously exacerbated as provincial governments seek to take a larger section of the economic pie for themselves, even when these efforts are strongly opposed by the federal government. Regional variations in evaluating foreign investment and U.S. multinationals, and in enacting policies and regulations that affect them, greatly heighten the complexities of MNC operations in Canada, and increase the uncertainties of doing business there.

North vs. South in Italy

The regional issue has been less salient in Italy, but is likely to become much more so in the future. The problem of the south—the Mezzogiorno—of course has been a major source of tension since the formation of the Italian state. Although four of the U.S. corporations that participated in our study have installations south of Rome, Italian government efforts to attract investment, foreign or domestic, there have not been spectacularly successful. A recent estimate puts the total of foreign capital located in the south at not more than ten percent of the total.[4]

Even more distressing perhaps is evidence that what Italians call rip-off investments *(investimenti di rapina)* have often occurred in the south. In 1976, the furor that raged around "Harry's Moda," an American soft goods firm whose closing meant the loss of over 3,000 jobs, served to heighten Italian antagonisms toward American companies, most of which have impeccable records as employers.

One of Italy's most radical, articulate and effective trade union leaders summarizes the problem this way:

"The motivations that brought industrial enterprises and speculators into southern Italy were of the meanest kind. The policies and the laws were so badly drafted, it was possible for an enterprise to come into southern Italy to establish a minimum facility largely through the use of credit facilities provided by the state, to make a quick profit and, as soon as circumstances turned bad, to abandon the place."

Few of those we interviewed mention the disparity between foreign investment inputs north and south. But our interviews were carried out in Rome, Bologna, Turin and Milan. It is certain that local elites at places like Bari, Naples or Catania would repeat what southern Italians have been saying for over a century; policies of the national government encourage, sometimes guarantee, the perpetuation of the great discrepancy between the economic development of the two areas of the Peninsula.

Even when U.S. foreign investment in the Italian south is not of the rip-off variety, Italians complain that American firms do not bring the very latest technology. The American food industry is frequently criticized on this score. One of our respondents, a leading figure in Italy's most important agricultural associations, says in this regard:

[4] There are conflicts about all such estimates. The Confidustria study (cited in note 1, p. 25) takes a more optimistic view. Although only about 19 percent of the 295 firms studied in 1971 were in the South and islands, the authors claim that many of the firms located in Lazio are in fact "south of Rome" and were often launched under the government's program to encourage southern investment (see pp. 13-16 of their study). Southerners are unlikely to accept this reasoning. They will note instead that over 80 percent of the firms are *not* in the south and that almost 60 percent of them are in the Industrial Triangle bounded by Genoa, Milan and Turin.

"We hold that an industry that wants to come here must use the same methods that are used in the United States. Certainly in some cases, particularly when we are talking about agricultural machinery, there will be the problem of adaptation to our local conditions. What I mean is that if industries come to us from your country and abjectly, as well as opportunistically, conform to what exists here, then believe me nothing changes."

Other Italian respondents suggest that future investment negotiations will involve regional political authorities. A present and a former president of two different regions north of Rome assure us that regional governments will play an increasingly central role on policies of land use, credit and tax facilitations, and agricultural and industrial development.

The above applies not only to those firms that may wish to enter Italy, but also to those that are in that country now. The point is that many Italians who clamor for a stronger national policy on multinationals also believe that such a policy should provide a prominent role for regional public authorities. One of the regions has already created a special agency to deal with the full range of problems pertaining to industrial and economic development. The agency's director, a Communist, expects to be negotiating directly with multinational managers in the immediate future.

Changes in 1973

Events of 1973 heightened concern with MNC's in both countries. Earlier Canadian attention, as seen, was more directed to manufacturing and the impact of foreign investment on that sector of the economy. The Gray Report and similar studies did mention that foreign investment in Canada also led to *more* resource extraction and *less* upgrading of raw materials before export than was desirable. But raw materials producers outside central Canada sometimes took the view that the real aim of Toronto nationalists was that of replacing U.S. ownership and control in Canada with their own.

Canadians we interviewed suggest that Canada will have to face the issue of foreign ownership and control in its natural resource sector much more directly than in the past. Although steps to control the export of raw materials have been taken, many Canadians feel that the development of a national policy for resources has become one of the nation's primary and most pressing tasks. External demands for Canadian resources have risen rapidly, far more than for Canadian manufactured goods. This gives rise to concerns that Canada is in danger of falling back into its traditional role of a supplier of raw materials to the developed parts of the world.

This situation does not always produce the same sense of dependency. Several of our respondents, reflecting recent Canadian assertiveness (as well as world events since 1973), see that the nation's vast natural resources provide it with a major instrument of international power. A manager of one U.S.-owned firm with substantial interests in Canadian agriculture observes that food production "is the power politics of the future and Canada is a superpower in food production." On the other hand, Canadians have been deeply disappointed to learn that initial estimates of the extent of the nation's petroleum resources seem to have been far too high, and that Canada will soon become a net importer of oil rather than a supplier.

It is difficult to say whether the traditional Canadian "psychology of dependency" has increased or decreased in the last few years. Canada, especially under the present government, has attempted more than ever before to create a distinct national identity and role for itself. Inevitably, these efforts—whether to assert its "cultural sovereignty," to exercise greater control over foreign investment, or to develop new relations with Western Europe and Japan—have made Canadian-U.S. relations more difficult. Yet, many Canadians (and some Americans, too) believe that a Canada that is more confident of its independence will be better able to take part in mutually beneficial endeavors with the United States.

Events of 1973 traumatized Italians as well. Even more so, perhaps, in view of Italy's massive dependence on energy sources located outside her borders. The issue of petroleum does not involve nationalization. Italian respondents, including Communist leaders without exception, indicate little interest in extending public ownership beyond the 40 percent of the market that the government now controls. Two respondents, however, predict that the petroleum industry will be scapegoated, and that not even the Communist party will be able to resist populist demands for nationalization. These demands should reach a crescendo if and when Italy's policy of providing energy at low cost (and therefore at enormous losses for the government and the oil companies) changes. Such a change would presumably require that a system of administered prices for petroleum products function in Italy at least as well as it does in France or Britain. Its implication would be marked increases in the price of what the industry calls "downstream" products.

Beyond petroleum, though, Italians have begun to worry about the entire highly complicated and politicized problem of the country's future energy needs. No such discussion proceeds very far without raising the specter of multinational power—and particularly the power of the United States. Although Italians are not as deeply scared as Canadians by the "psychology of dependency," signs of it are there.

Chapter 4
Equity Ownership, Joint Ventures, and Control

CANADIANS disagree sharply on the steps that should be taken to deal with the problems associated with the presence of so many foreign-owned and controlled firms in the economy. Several of our respondents agree with a leading economist who states that:

"The major cause of Canadian problems in which U.S. firms appear to play such a major role is a more basic problem of Canadian economic and industrial policy —which has attracted too many firms, each of which produces too many products at too high a cost."

Respondents are divided, too, between those who underline the basic need to lower Canadian tariffs and those who point to the prior requirement of developing a clearly defined national industrial policy before the Canadian economy is opened to international competition.

The position that the government should change its traditional tariff, tax and competition policies is represented in Canada by such major organizations as the Economic Council of Canada and the Canadian-American Committee. The position has little political support at present, in large measure because of fears that lowering Canadian tariffs will lead to closer economic integration between Canada and the United States. Some feel, too, that closer economic integration necessarily implies greater integration in other areas—cultural, social and political.

Canadian Review of Foreign Investment

The majority of Canadians, however, do agree that the problems of foreign ownership and control in the economy should be treated either in conjunction with a freer trade policy or as a prior condition of it. Most of those we interviewed favor the present policy of screening incoming foreign direct investment. But whereas some believe that ownership in itself is not a critical factor to worry about, others are convinced that ownership is *the* vital issue and that the government should act directly to increase the level of Canadian ownership in the economy. This first view is mirrored in the following excerpt from the Gray Report:

"Canadian control of a business is not in itself a guarantee of sound performance and is not, therefore, a satisfactory means for achieving Canada's broad national objectives . . . . The Canadian government cannot be totally indifferent to country of control. In the main, however, Canadian ownership and control of business is not a sufficient answer to the problems which would remain after general and remedial policies were implemented." [1]

[1] *Foreign Direct Investment in Canada.* Ottawa: Government of Canada, 1972, pp. 437, 439.

Though the Foreign Investment Review Agency's (FIRA) mandate presently is quite narrow, the Agency in principle is to monitor continuously the plans of foreign direct investors, assure that existing investments are beneficial, and negotiate with them to increase Canadian benefits from these investments.[2] If necessary it can block foreign investment where it seems in the national interest to do so.

One of the five major criteria the Agency uses to evaluate the benefits of proposed investments refers to participation by Canadians in the management and operation of the enterprise but not, notably, in ownership. This approach agrees with the views of many of the elites interviewed. Their view is nicely put by a leader of the Canadian labor movement: "The ownership question is basically irrelevant." This outlook is strongest among administrative officials in the federal and the provincial governments, despite the federal-provincial tensions noted above.

One economist offers a reason for this enthusiasm expressed by government bureaucrats, and says:

"The screening process strengthens the hands of bureaucrats, by allowing them a wide range of administration discretion and bureaucratic involvement in these issues and thus is likely to be the type of approach which is attractive to the ministries and bureaucrats in government. . . . It places them in the center of the negotiating process."

As we shall see later, some Canadians would favor an even stronger selective and discretionary approach to government decisions on foreign investment and MNC's.

Canadians who believe that the basic question of ownership must be given first priority may be increasing. But this does not mean an increased interest in expanding public ownership in the economy. The Liberal and Conservative parties are both strongly opposed. The New Democratic Party (NDP) has consistently adopted the strongest party line toward foreign investment and MNC's, but it opposes demands for large-scale nationalization in the Canadian economy. Under its current leadership, it is more likely than ever to resist such a policy. A senior research officer of the NDP notes:

"The NDP does not favor nationalization of industry as an end or goal in itself, but rather seeks the development of a rational and overall national economic plan which rests on a clear industrial strategy."

Nor have Canadian trade unions showed any interest in public ownership.

One respondent, long associated with the notion of "repatriating" or "buying back" foreign-owned firms, recommends that the Canadian government "require

---

[2] The *Foreign Investment Review Act* (C.S. 1974,c.46) and its operative arm, the Foreign Investment Review Agency, were recommended initially in the Gray Report. The Act came into effect in 1974. The operations of the Agency were expanded in October, 1975.

the owners of the thirty largest Canadian subsidiaries to sell their firms to Canadian owners over a ten-year period." Another urges the restructuring of the Foreign Investment Review Agency to "create a situation in which the Canadian owner of a business has to have permission to sell out to a foreigner."

These views, like those on nationalization, find little support among our other respondents. But it is clear that the rapidly widening concern in Canada about the protection of its natural resources is likely to require government intervention in one way or another. The chief executive officer of a major oil company points, for example, to "the growing governmental involvement in Canada in the energy and oil industries, not in terms of nationalization or a buy-back policy . . . but in a variety of new joint ventures, such as Petro-Canada. . . ."

Pressure for more joint ventures of this type, while increasing, are still limited, however, to the natural resource sector and do not yet seem to represent a clearly defined policy by either the federal or provincial governments.

More significant for U.S. parent companies, perhaps, is the view of many, and particularly of Canadian executives of U.S. subsidiaries; they believe that a substantial degree of Canadian ownership is absolutely essential if U.S. MNC's are going to be responsive and responsible to the host country. A senior vice president of an American subsidiary of one of Canada's largest firms suggests that "the primary error U.S. firms make in their operations in Canada is to centralize decision making in the United States. The only solution for this and other problems is substantially increased Canadian ownership."

Another Canadian manager in a U.S.-owned firm states flatly that "the wholly owned subsidiary cannot be the best corporate citizen." His views were echoed by executives in several other companies; one of whom says:

"The wholly owned subsidiary cannot maximize decisions in the interests of the host country. Even a minority shareholding interest in the host country builds a countervailing force into the decision-making process of the subsidiary. This is the bare minimum that provides a voice within the firm, within the subsidiary, which speaks for Canadian interests."

It is noteworthy that among the firms in our survey which were evaluated by respondents as very good corporate citizens, almost all had some degree of Canadian equity ownership. In each case, the senior management of the subsidiary was well aware of the advantages this provided for the company in its dealings with its parent. These respondents recognize the technical difficulties in restructuring a wholly owned subsidiary to include a degree of Canadian equity ownership; but they also emphasize that the end is well worth the difficulties involved.

Several other respondents say this approach would involve "a waste of Canadian capital." A Canadian economist and a leading figure in one of the major political parties meets this criticism head-on. He suggests that given the alternative uses to which Canadian capital would otherwise be put, this was scarcely the worst. He is prepared to recommend that the Canadian government require that foreign-owned firms make at least minority, and perhaps even majority, holdings

Table 4-1: Ownership Patterns of Affiliates of U.S. Multinational Corporations (by year and geographic area; in percent, 187 firms)

Area	Wholly Owned 1939	1957	1967	Not Wholly Owned* 1939	1957	1967	Unknown 1939	1957	1967
Canada	78.5	79.7	78.0	9.1	11.7	13.8	12.5	8.5	8.2
EC	59.5	60.9	61.2	25.4	26.2	29.2	15.1	13.0	9.7

* Includes both minority and majority local interests

Source: United Nations Organization, *Multinational Corporations in World Development.* ST/ECA/190, 1973, pp. 156-57.

available to Canadians. He says that these shares would not *necessarily* be acquired by Canadians, but rather that the *opportunity* for Canadian equity participation must be made available.

It may be that an additional reason Canadians are thinking more about joint equity ownership is that so few foreign firms there involve local minority or majority participation. In the countries encompassed by the European Communities, governments and local capital interests have been more effective than Canadians in bringing about shared ownership. In fact, the difference between Canada and Europe on this score has remained extremely stable over a period of almost forty years, as Table 4-1 shows.

The Italian Perspective

Italian respondents less frequently raise issues touching on equity ownership and joint ventures. The scale of public-sector involvement in the Italian economy far exceeds that in Canada, and even leaders of the Communist Party in Italy take pains to emphasize that they do not look to any further expansion of public ownership. The Communist position, though more fully developed, is similar to the NDP position in Canada.

There are also interesting parallels in the two countries in the growing interest in the possibilities and value of joint ventures between the host government and U.S. MNC's, particularly in the energy field. A senior Italian manager of a large number of manufacturing enterprises in the public sector suggests a range of joint-venture possibilities between U.S. MNC's and Italian industries in the public sector, involving collaboration in both the Third World and in Italy. Similarly, an Italian economist expresses the unusual but interesting opinion that:

"The large-scale multinationals in Italy increasingly perfer to deal with the Italian state and not with the private sector. These large-scale firms might even like to deal with governmental agencies running nationalized industries and to enter into joint ventures with them."

A respondent from a major agricultural association suggests that Italy's agricultural regions would provide unusually attractive opportunities for U.S. investors.

He believes that there would be exceptional opportunities for joint ventures and for support from national and regional governments in the establishment of enterprises furnishing agricultural chemicals and machinery. Agricultural regions, he says, deeply need the kind of revolutionary machinery that American companies have pioneered. He concludes: "If you Americans believe that the political side of Italy is important, then I can assure you this is the moment to invest and not to run away from this country."

Another respondent, however, says that while the practice of joint ventures has given good results, he doubts that U.S. MNC's will be attracted by them. "I know that often the multinationals don't want to enter into these arrangements," he says. Nevertheless, as in Canada, pressures as well as opportunities for U.S. firms to form joint ventures with both private business and with the public sector—especially in the energy sector—seem likely to increase in the foreseeable future. But there is no clearly formulated policy on joint ventures in either country at the present time.

Although Italians do not raise the issue of joint ventures as often as do Canadians, the issue is very close to the surface of a good deal of elite thinking. They express the belief that American firms generally resist these arrangements. An economist, however, expresses concern that joint ventures might contaminate the affiliate by introducing exactly those aspects of industrial management in Italy that the wholly owned American subsidiary manages to avoid. A national minister, on the other hand, argues that a little more joint venture will help to reduce American management's tendency to want to overadminister local situations from the United States.

A former Italian minister, a leading industrialist, and a newspaper editor spontaneously come up with an interesting twist on the joint-venture issue. They suggest that the United States, in terms of restrictions on foreign investment at home, is much less liberal than its public pronouncements about international trade and investment might suggest. They note, for example, that the United States becomes an increasingly attractive place for European investors, and that these latter might be interested in more joint or wholly owned ventures in the United States. The industrialist in particular believes that the genuine internationalization of industrial enterprise would imply joint-venture arrangements of a broad, reciprocal kind.

An Italian CEO of a U.S. affiliate adds that not merely joint ventures but "going public" in Italy is the way of the future. He believes U.S. firms will probably have to accept minority, and in some cases majority, local equity participation as a condition for doing business locally.

Finally, we might note here that many Italian respondents—particularly party leaders, bureaucrats and trade unionists—who want more effective controls of multinationals have been in touch with Japanese and Canadians. It seems likely that Canadian initiatives in the joint venture matter would be well received by these Italians.

Chapter 5
Research and Development

Mᴏʀᴇ ᴛʜᴀɴ research and development, no area of U.S.-MNC activity is so widely considered in Canada to illustrate the problem of "truncation." Canadians by and large believe that the lack of sufficient research and development activities is the most outstanding failure of U.S. firms in Canada. They say that the lack of indigenous research and development capacity in Canada is perhaps the clearest indication of Canadian dependence on the United States. Views of our respondents on this topic simply confirm what many Canadian reports and studies of recent years have concluded.[1]

There are those who do not agree with these views. An adviser to the government on industrial matters, for example, suggests that there is considerable value for Canada "in buying research and development that others, particularly the United States, have done. It is cheaper and lessens risks in the purchasing country." This view is echoed by an Italian economist who believes that the more flexible and successful MNC's of the future will be those that become specialized in the purchase and adaptation of technologies to the conditions of given countries.

Others, who are less critical, note that the level of research and development carried on by U.S. subsidiaries in Canada is significantly higher than that carried on by Canadian-owned firms. The critics reply, however, that more recent studies show that this is no longer the case, and they portray a decline in the research and development carried on by U.S. firms in Canada. In any case, they say, it is scarcely surprising that U.S.-owned firms have carried on more research than Canadian, given that U.S. ownership tends to be more extensive in the high-technology industries.

Indigenous Canadian business leaders differ considerably in their evaluations of this matter. The chief executive officer of a large Canadian-owned firm says: "I deplore the fact that more research and development is not done in Canada." He

---

[1] See, for example, Arthur J. Cordell, *The Multinational Firm, Foreign Direct Investment, and Canadian Science Policy*. Ottawa: Science Council of Canada, 1971; and *Innovation in a Cold Climate: The Dilemma of Canadian Manufacturing*. Ottawa: Science Council of Canada, 1971; *Report of the Select Committee on Economic and Cultural Nationalism, Final Report*. Toronto: Queen's Printer for Ontario, 1975, Chapter 3; *Foreign Direct Investment in Canada*. Ottawa: Government of Canada, 1972, Chapter 8; and A. E. Safarian, *The Performance of Foreign-Owned Firms in Canada*. Montreal: Private Planning Association of Canada, 1969, Chapter 5.

The Conference Board, in cooperation with the National Science Foundation, recently completed a major survey of overseas R and D by U.S. multinationals. The survey reports that U.S. multinationals expanded their overseas research programs abroad at a much more rapid pace than at home during the late 1960's and early 1970's. Between 1970 and 1975, survey results suggest that there was little real growth in R and D expenditures by U.S. foreign affiliates. See Daniel Creamer, *Overseas Research and Development by United States Multinationals, 1966-1975: Estimates of Expenditures and a Statistical Profile*. The Conference Board, Report No. 685, 1976, especially Chapters 4, 5 and 6.

believes that it is difficult to fault the MNC directly because centralized research and development is normally more economical for the firm. He adds: "Even though it will cost more, foreign-owned firms should and could do more research and development in Canada."

The director of a major trade association states that "the Gray Report was basically correct, especially with regard to research and development." On the other hand, executives of other industrial organizations suggest that the lack of research and development by U.S. MNC's, while important, is not a vital criticism of their operations in Canada.

Research, Development, and National Status

Although these quoted passages may sound evenly balanced, that is not how Canadian views in this matter are distributed. In the popular mind, but especially in the perceptions of strategic Canadian elites, the American parent does not organize or permit as much research and development in their country as they think essential. The fact that they generally do not present strong technical arguments or evidence that this is so does not make the perceptions and criticisms less important.

To many Canadians, low levels of indigenous research and development capability symbolize a second-rate status for the nation. As one Canadian intellectual puts it: Great Powers possess technological sovereignty. They also lead in design capability. For these nations, national scientific objectives, like reaching the moon, can be independently set and realized. And he quotes Professor Robert Gilpin:

"Today Great Power status accrues to those nations which are leaders in all phases of basic research and which possess financial and managerial means to convert new knowledge into advanced technologies. . . . It appears most unlikely that any nation . . . can ever again aspire to a dominant role in international politics without possessing a strong, indigenous scientific and technological capacity. International politics has passed from the era of traditional, industrial nation-states to one dominated by the scientific nation-states."[2]

Few Canadian elites aspire to Great Power status for Canada. But Great Power status is one thing and dependence another and, for many, "technological sovereignty" is the cornerstone of national independence.

In Italy, too, there are frequent attacks on American firms for their alleged failure to perform more research and development. Even those who express the most favorable views toward American capital believe that more could be done to improve the indigenous research capability of U.S. affiliates, thereby benefiting the country as a whole.

A leading Italian economist states that all of the data available on local investment "systematically show that the economic impact of multinationals in Italy has

---

[2] Robert Gilpin, *France in the Age of the Scientific State*. Princeton, N.J.: Princeton University Press, 1968, p.25. See also David H. Blake and R. S. Walters, *The Politics of Global Economic Relations*. Englewood Cliffs: Prentice-Hall, 1976, Chapter 10.

been positive." He then continues that "the only strongly supported objective criticism that one can make of the multinationals in Italy (and particularly American multinationals) is that they have not brought very much research and development to the country."

An Italian industrialist states that a "basic accusation" against some U.S. MNC's is that: "They come to Italy and they permit the affiliates to engage in all kinds of work associated with the enterprise, except research and development."

A former minister in the Italian government underlines the belief that: "Italy is really less dependent on the multinational firm as such, than it is dependent on a certain lack of indigenous technology and know-how." But dependency in these terms is not the same as in Canada. Research and development is a "dimension of multinational operations in this country that is badly lacking," a former high government official observes, but this does not give rise to the same concerns about national autonomy and independence as in Canada.

Italians, like Canadians, understand the logic of multinational enterprise and understand that in some cases these organizations do indeed upgrade the local research capability. An Italian manager of a U.S.-owned firm with an exceptionally favorable research and development image says: "The fundamental question about foreign investment is whether it increases the know-how available in a country." On the whole he believes that U.S. firms are better at this than Italian firms because the former generally invest more not only in research and development but in market analysis and planning, too.

An economist agrees that this is so. He adds though that Italians, like other Europeans, recognize that, especially regarding research, parent companies can and do make highly arbitrary decisions to place the function wherever central management may prefer. They often do this without regard to what may be the impact of these decisions on a host country.[3]

Italians also express a dilemma and attitude about research and development that is typical on the Continent. On the one hand, Italy manifests a nationalistic desire to develop a research and development capability in its own right. Like other European countries, Italy has been tempted to develop "national champions" in the industrial area.

But, as several of our respondents note, there are basic industrial sectors, vital to Italian security and defense and to her future development, where there is no chance at all that the nation could develop a viable research and development presence. The sectors that keep coming up for mention in this context are aerospace, computers, electronics, petroleum and nuclear energy. Additionally, some Italians mention natural resource exploration as requiring more financial and human resources than Italy can provide.

For most who comment in this vein the answer is some form of collaboration at the Western European system level. They add, however, that even such collabora-

---

[3] For the most useful treatment of the major aspects of direct foreign investment in Italy, see Part V, "Investimenti esteri diretti e impresa multinazionale," in Franco Momigliano, *Economia industriale e teoria dell'impresa*. Bologna: Il Mulino, 1975, pp. 365-463.

tive efforts can be defeated by decisions based on nationalistic, or "national champion," considerations. The fate of French-English collaboration on the Concorde is the cited example.

At least one Italian criticism differs sharply from any made in Canada. Several respondents allege that U.S. firms have "killed off" ongoing research and development operations after taking over an Italian firm. After the take-over, one individual noted:

"In the Italian plant, there was no room at all for research. Our engineers had to go back to school. What happened is that _____ actually killed off the research division, even though there were men of high quality around. The engineers preferred to go back to the university as assistants, at one-third their wages, to remaining in a place where they could do no research."

Trade unionists in particular claim that the first step that follows an American take-over is the termination of on-site research. It is possible that two or three notorious cases—one of them at Naples involving a firm's "dismantling" a bogus research and development division created just before the plant was sold to American interests—have been confused with many times that number. Nevertheless instances such as these combine with clear-cut cases of very little decentralized research work to convince Italians that this aspect of foreign industrial investment may carry more cost than benefit.

The chief executive officer of a U.S.-owned manufacturing company in Canada—one of the largest firms in the country—observed that his organization, which does almost no research in Canada, feels "considerable pressure on the research side, and Canadians would like to have more research in the industry carried on in Canada." But, he adds: "If we did more research here it would not add to the economic benefit of the country. It is not a question of where the research is done but a question of what research is done and whether the firms in Canada have economic access to this research."

Many Canadians would respond that it is a question not only of *economic* benefit, but of *political* and *cultural* "benefits" as well. However, the quotation does raise the important issue that the site of research is only one aspect in its availability.

The Science Council of Canada, for example, identifies two primary types of research and development operations carried on by foreign subsidiaries in Canada. One is the "international interdependent laboratory," which conducts research with little development and is tightly integrated into the parent firm's international research program. The second is the "support laboratory," which acts as a technical service center and serves as the "translator" of foreign technology for the host country." [4]

The first type of research operation, the Council suggests, may offer little or no actual benefits to the country. If its research is linked to the parent firm's

---

[4] Cordell, *op. cit.,* pp. 43-46.

international research program and not to the ongoing activities of the Canadian subsidiary, it might provide employment benefits for a few highly skilled Canadians and result in the upgrading of the skills of a few more, but the spillover effect to Canada may well be minimal. It is possible for a research and development operation in a host country to be limited to purely applied developmental tasks, and thus serve a minimal function in technology transfer. It is also possible for a research operation to be too concerned with advanced research and fail to provide any meaningful benefits for the host country.

In a nutshell the argument is that research and development must be carried on in the right place and on the right matters. The real question is not so much *whether* there is research and development in some form, but *who determines* what form it shall take. On this, both Italians and Canadians agree.

Developing Local Products and Markets

A number of Canadians with whom we spoke are sharply critical of U.S. multinationals' research and development policies along just these lines. They are particularly exercised over instances of U.S. parents refusing to permit Canadian subsidiaries to develop specialized products which would be internationally competitive, or to take full responsibility, from research through to export, for a particular product line.

Several different although related issues were raised in these discussions. Executives of one subsidiary express extreme unhappiness that their parent organization refused to permit them to develop a new product line based on unique Canadian conditions which, they believe, would have an internationally competitive potential. The parent firm, a relatively small American MNC, insisted instead that the Canadian subsidiary continue to concentrate on the main line of products which it had traditionally offered on the international market.

Canadian subsidiaries of a considerable number of U.S. firms, including one participating in our study, have full responsibility for a particular product line. The basic issue in these situations is whether, through the firm's integration into an international production system, the operation of the subsidiary in Canada has any significant autonomy, either in research, development or marketing—especially if its exports are all designated for subsidiaries of the same company in other countries.

In this the trade-offs for the host country can be difficult. The subsidiary may perform advanced research and development; it may have clear independent responsibilities for certain products or components; and it may be a substantial exporter. Yet, it might still be a "truncated" enterprise, over which the host government can exercise little effective control. Indeed, in certain operations like this, the technological development of the host country can actually be held back.

An Italian respondent, a journalist, comments that "the know-how (unless it is transferred to the host country) can actually keep the host country in a state of dependency and inhibit its own autonomous development." He states that, in one particular field, Italy's dependence on outside MNC's, especially U.S. MNC's, "has actually cut the country's development short." He adds: "In effect, with the exception of some production of the more marginally important ____ goods, Italy simply engages in assembly of products . . . the technology of which is located outside of Italy.''

On a similar note are the comments of two other Italians who manage American multinationals. One of them, whose company does have full-scale international responsibility for a particular product line, emphasizes that the mandate includes unfettered decisions as to research and development, but strictly in the product line prescribed in the United States. What is developed in Italy, however, is sold everywhere in the world where the parent company has marketing arrangements.

The other executive claims that the only way to operate is to give any and every subsidiary authority to engage in research and development. The subsidiary should be able to put its research ideas out for bids to other units of the company (including the parent!). The fruits of research and development are then shared with company units that invest in them. Units that do not share the research and development risk pay royalties. He adds that arguments about critical mass and economies of scale in research and development are largely spurious.

A senior executive in one of the Canadian subsidiaries in our study summarizes these views with the statement that the most appropriate industrial policy for Canada would be one that encourages within multinational enterprises ''the development of particular technologies which would make Canada world competitive in these fields.'' Another high-level manager of a U.S.-owned firm in Canada sees this as a much more gradual process. The development of worldwide competitiveness in a few product lines, he says, is still ''too much a theory'' given Canada's relatively low level of industrialization. He asks: ''Why would anyone invest in Canada—to serve a world market?'' He, too, however, sees the development of unique Canadian products which will compete on an international scale as the longer term goal of Canadian industrial policy.

Still another manager states that one remedy for Canada's ''branch plant economy'' is ''to provide specialized research and development responsibility for Canadian subsidiaries.'' His company, an affiliate of an American firm widely considered in Canada to be among the best corporate citizens, has long had full international responsibility for several of the firm's products.

It is interesting that in each of the above four cases the managers of U.S. subsidiaries anticipate that there would have to be close cooperation between the firms and the Canadian government to identify and develop such specialized product lines. One of them, reflecting on an admittedly controversial topic, says:

''The Canadian government should play a more innovative sponsoring role in the identification of areas for concentration and innovation. It should make funds available and indeed even remain, if necessary, to provide the core of the operation once development has been undertaken.''

This discussion obviously leads to more general issues involving alternative forms of multinational organization, and the implications for MNC's of changing relations between public and private sectors in advanced industrial nations. These issues will be considered in Chapter 13.

Additional criticisms and concerns about the research and development policies of U.S. MNC's were raised in both countries. An official in the government reiterated a complaint heard widely in Canada, namely, that the products of U.S. subsidiaries in Canada are rarely adapted to particular Canadian tastes or requirements. "Subsidiaries copy all too readily the product range and production techniques of U.S. firms. . . . This undermines the creative dimension in Canadian industry."

Many respondents repeated the familiar saw: "The Canadian product is the American one, but $20 more expensive." Complaints were not limited to research and development in production. Canadians lament, too, the failure of U.S. firms in Canada to carry on more marketing research and to develop Canadian-oriented marketing programs.

The cost of research and development is questioned by several respondents. Two Italians question whether profits earned in Italy should go to finance research and development by the MNC in another country or in the United States. "Does this or does it not involve a transfer of capital?" one of them asks. The idea that in the long run everyone benefits from the results of exploration, research and development does not impress or convince many Italian elites, with the qualified exception of the economists in our sample. Even here, an economist who has been, and will again be, a major influence on policy is quite explicit: What justifies a multinational presence in Italy, he believes, is the "scientific and technological fallout." Where that is lacking, costs outweigh benefits.

Similar pressures are felt in Canada from the federal government. An American manager in a firm which is highly research intensive says that it faces "continued and increasing pressure . . . to expand our manufacturing and research facilities in the country." Some government officials, he adds, "would like to work this out by a strict quantitative formula; they would like to see Canada have a research facility that is equivalent to the percentage of —————'s sales in the country."

Italians also call attention to the time lag in the transfer of technology from the United States. Products and technology allegedly arrive in Italy after they appear in the United States. One respondent, a former senior government official, observes that U.S. companies frequently send their obsolete machinery to Italy. Two others say that American food processing companies, in particular, have failed to bring Italy the most up-to-date technologies in the industry.

This is clearly not a simple problem for U.S. multinationals. The European Regional Director of a U.S. firm says that his organization has not suffered much criticism because of its failure to do more research and development in Europe. He says that the firm is "much more concerned with criticism in the United States that they would be exporting technological jobs than with complaints in Western Europe about its research and development policies."

Opportunities for R and D Personnel

Canadians and Italians are also preoccupied about jobs for indigenous scientific and technical personnel. United States multinationals are expected by them to provide more employment opportunities for scientists, research workers, and technicians. A Canadian expert reports that a recent study he has carried out shows that there has been substantial general decline in employment opportunities in industry for Canadian scientists and engineers. The idea is that there would be more such jobs if more MNC-related research were located in Canada.

In both countries, respondents add that the relationship between universities and multinational enterprises is far from ideal. Somehow, American firms are asked to succeed where Italy or Canada itself has failed. Affiliates are called on to stimulate greater interest in technological innovation in national universities by expanding their local research and development operations. An Italian professor of economics urges that the U.S. multinationals ''pay more attention than they have to the brain-draining consequences of how they operate in Italy and in other European countries.''

Several younger Canadian scientists and engineers add that they do not want to leave the country, but that the centralized research and development policies of the U.S. firms they work for gives them no other choice but to transfer to the United States if they wish to advance their careers.

Adequacy of National Science Policies

Finally, our respondents in both countries highlight the inadequacies of national science policies. The failure of both countries to develop a more satisfactory national approach to research and development is said to make them far more vulnerable to the impact of existing multinational research and development policies. This hiatus in national policy also means that governments will have less than desirable leverage in their dealings with foreign firms.

After enumerating a variety of criticisms turning on research and development, an Italian economist observes: ''In my opinion, these criticisms are really of the Italian government. If there were a policy, then more control of investment, more control of the restructuring of industry would take place.''

In Canada, one of the criteria used by the Foreign Investment Review Agency to evaluate proposals for direct investment is ''the effect of the acquisition or establishment on productivity, industrial efficiency, technological development, product innovation, and product variety in Canada.'' But few Canadians feel that this has had any impact on research and development thus far. Many continue to criticize the government for its failure to act more directly to increase the amount of research and development undertaken in the country. It is probable that similar future pressures on the Italian government will be even more insistent and severe.

Chapter 6
The Politics of Disinvestment

To DISINVEST is not only a momentous decision for the business enterprise; it can have traumatic effects in the host country as well. Thus the second most frequent criticism Italian elites voice about multinationals is that numbers of them are abandoning Italy. Many of those interviewed believe that this abandonment— *politica di disimpegno* as the Italians call it—is a matter of deliberate U.S. *governmental* policy. Some claim that both the U.S. government and the American industrial community are using some of these bail-outs as a warning to Italians not to support the Communist party. If nothing else, the electoral results of June, 1976, will have suggested that any such effort, real or imagined, was largely lost on the Italian voter.

Are MNC's Leaving Italy?

How important is this problem? The issue is marginal in terms of the more than two thousand foreign affiliates (about 700 of them American) operating in Italy. Officials of the U.S. government in Italy, representatives of the Chamber of Commerce of the United States in Italy, and of U.S. affiliates underscore that not more than about twenty U.S. firms have bailed out or are seriously considering doing so. More than balancing this prospect are often extensive plans by U.S. companies, including several we studied, to increase their investment commitments in Italy.

Nevertheless, events of recent years have brought Italians up short. Some of the most severe critics of multinational corporations have now become the loudest complainers about the alleged "politics of disinvestment." As one writer put it: "Those who yesterday were yelling 'Yankees Go Home!' are today the first to lament the exodus of multinationals when it occurs." The exodus of major firms like British Petroleum and Shell Oil, Singer and Leyland-Innocenti, General Instruments and Ducati-Thomson, Lepetit-Dow and Richardson-Merrell does not go unnoticed. Actual cases of partial or total abandonment lead to rumors that a general exodus is under way. The growing sense of anger and panic can be gleaned from newspaper headlines such as these:

"Where Is Foreign Capital Going?"
"Como Is Worried about Multinational Closing"
"The Multinationals Are Abandoning Us"
"They Are Closing Down"
"Panic Among Multinationals Abandoning Italy En Masse"
"Why the Multinationals Are Leaving Italy"

American firms are held particularly responsible for this, even though the pull-out involves firms from many nations.

Extensive media coverage of actual and threatened abandonment has varied effects in Italy. For example it serves to underscore what many of our respondents identify as the striking difference between a national and multinational firm— namely, the ability of the latter to pull out when the going gets rough, or when closing down represents a rational or optimal corporate decision. One of Italy's high-level bureaucrats says about this: "They want equal treatment here and also want the unequal opportunity to get out."

It is fair to say that elites pretty much across the board are somewhat disgruntled about this. Many of them underscore this multinational option as evidence that the multinational corporation is a highly independent, dispassionate and somewhat cold-blooded organization that takes decisions without regard to local needs, with an eye exclusively to the overarching profit motive. In the words of a leading intellectual and former member of parliament:

"Can you ask a businessman to worry about a country's welfare? Can you ask him to come into a country and then not to pull out if he is not making money? Remember that no local businessman has this ability and can act quite so cold-bloodedly. When the multinationals do this, it creates a trauma; people feel let down. If the multinational has been successful and made money in the past, this makes its leaving an even more embittering experience. The more a multinational has done for a country, the greater the bitterness when it decides to leave."

Left-wing critics of the multinationals carry the argument further. They create images of gigantic corporations—usually American—served by equally gigantic computers and instantaneous worldwide communications systems in their decision-making. However far-fetched the idea may be that plants are built and closed, production and sales plans formed, modified and abandoned at a moment's notice, that is part of the picture created in Italy—and accepted to some extent by Italy's elites. The multinational's decision to stay or leave is depicted as governed by short- and medium-term considerations of labor costs, trained manpower, capital markets, and other factors that go into profit-maximizing strategies. At the extreme, a Communist newspaper like *Unità* (December 28, 1975, p. 14) will describe all of this as an example of how about 200 U.S. firms from the *Fortune* list, controlling three-fourths of U.S. direct investment abroad, become the monopolistic arm of American imperialism.

Labor Costs a Problem

Because the issue of abandonment came up so frequently in the interviews, the respondents were asked why they thought this was happening, whether it was justifiable, and what might be done about it. Members of the U.S. government community in Italy underscore Italy's economic downturn, the high cost of Italian labor, and the attractiveness of investment opportunities in the Third World as reasons for some American—and European—firms leaving Italy. One official says:

"Let's face it; corporations often came to Italy because of the relatively low labor costs here that would give them a margin on the world market. Now the situation has turned and the companies are having more than a little trouble deciding whether to stay or pull out. The unions have brought things around to the point where businesses find it more and more difficult to operate at a profit. The basic problem with Italy today is that people are no longer willing to accept the idea that if a firm is going to stay in business it has to make a profit."

Most of the Italians interviewed recognize that the cost of labor in Italy is a major problem. The secretary general of one political party says: "Italy no longer represents labor-cost advantages. Productivity being what it is, why should a multinational that depends in large measure on the cost of labor be interested in remaining in this country?" A leading Italian industrialist adds that if Italian firms could get out and go elsewhere they, too, would do so. The difference between them and the multinationals, he adds, is that the Italian companies *have* to continue to negotiate with the unions and the government until the very last moment. These protracted negotiations are extremely costly; in many cases they conclude by having the profitless plant turned over to one public agency or another.

However, this respondent (and other Italians as well) adds that multinational decisions to close down or to sell out are often entirely too precipitous. Because local managers may not understand the realities of Italian politics and of Italian industrial relations, wrong decisions based on distorted or erroneous information may be taken. "The local affiliates often depend too much on decisions of the parent companies, and the parent companies often do not comprehend that Italy is simply *not* a place where many of these things or problems can be settled in a week."

This point was also stressed by a U.S. Embassy official, who has had direct experience in helping to prevent the departure from Italy of at least one U.S. firm. He comments: "Top managers at home often don't realize that when Italian trade union leaders say that *nothing* is negotiable what they really mean is that *everything* is negotiable. The trick is to find the way without causing loss of face."

The Italian economists interviewed are entirely aware of the logic and the pressures that lead to disinvestment decisions. One of them says: "They run because they cannot tolerate losses, except for a limited and roughly predictable period. These multinationals are not politically tied to the territory. They follow a logic that is easy enough to comprehend." Another adds that while the departure of many multinationals from Italy is both impressive and depressing, he does not anticipate that much can be done to reduce the cost of Italian labor. He adds that these departures clearly add to negative opinions held regarding foreign firms. He expects as well that, if such departures continue, the government will have to step in to make them less likely—or at least much more difficult—in the years ahead. He adds:

"We have a Minister of Industry who everyday these days is living with dozens of threatened closings. He is wasting a lot of time functioning as a mediator, rather than worrying about articulating an industrial policy for the country. Sheer madness! What we are going to get if this continues is an anti-liberal legislative proposal, and curiously enough it will be supported by sectors of Italian society that didn't earlier support such proposals. I suspect that what we will get is a new kind of national solidarity against multinationals.

"If there were in Italy a Committee of the Middle Class (and there isn't naturally), the Committee would no doubt say to the multinationals that they should avoid actions that reverberate negatively for the whole multinational community."

Even Communist Party economists who are willing to acknowledge the profit motive, and who agree that something must be done to cope with the soaring cost of labor and welfare payments in Italy, add that foreign firms cannot be permitted to cut bait abruptly, or to "toss workers out on the street, like so many sacks of garbage." They add that the multinationals must learn to be more judicious and self-restrained in the use of their undoubted ability to get out. They echo the views of several Italian trade union leaders and industrial managers who say that in troubled times plant managers and worker representatives understand that they must live together and search out mutually acceptable solutions and compromises for common problems. Trade unionists in particular insist that nothing stands in the way of multinational affiliates following the same bargaining strategies, and reaching for the same kinds of accommodating solutions, that are typical of local firms. The one exception, of course, would be the bail-out procedure involving public sector take-over, but presumably foreign firms would wish to avoid this anyway.

Union leaders as a group suggest that managers of multinational affiliates are not as able to maneuver and to play the Italian game as are the managers of indigenous industries. However, this criticism should be reviewed against what we report on the patterns of management of American firms in Italy and Canada (see pages 55 to 66).

The Industrial Relations Climate

Trade union leaders also express the suspicion and fear that a major factor leading multinationals to abandon Italy is the system of industrial relations that prevails there. Some of them say that, where that is the case, the MNC may wish to leave the country, and perhaps should.

One of them adds, however, that there are instances where companies claiming to lose money not only wish to leave Italy but also refuse to sell their plants on the ground that this would create unwanted competition for them on the Italian market. This, he suggests, is going too far and is unacceptable. Several other respondents made the same point, referring to an actual case where Italian and American officials, American company representatives, and trade unionists were grappling with such a problem.

Reasonably typical of the trade union attitude toward abandonment is the following angry comment by one of Italy's major union leaders:

"Look, let's face the fact that most multinationals are less interested in what you are calling social responsibility than they are interested in immediate profits. This is especially so if they can get the hell out in a hurry whenever they want to. They come here and set up operations. But as soon as the trade unions arrived they wound up transferring the plant—to Formosa for example.

"I do not believe that international firms can consider Italy a land to be abandoned. There are good political as well as economic reasons for this. In a situation where your Department of State cannot send cannons or warships to Italy, its best possibility is to try to maintain an economic presence. This is what I expect will happen; I am not concerned that large-scale multinational firms will abandon us."

This last view is a minority view among those we interviewed. Most Italians do, indeed, feel that there will be more departures—not merely of American but of French, German, Swiss and English firms as well. In all probability, as an Italian economist puts it, these will be relatively few and perhaps the relatively larger of the multinational companies. He adds that when people think about multinationals they tend to think of IBM and Exxon. But he feels that the many smaller, less visible, more flexible multinationals in his country experience much less difficulty, and display much less propensity to leave the Italian scene. All of the fuss, he says, is, after all, concentrated on the visible part of the multinational iceberg.

The Large and the Small Multinationals

Others we interviewed believe that the top of the iceberg profoundly determines what impression people and policy makers have of the thing as a whole. They add that the smaller companies may be led to imitate what the large companies do. They believe, too, as one person put it, that for Italy to lose an Exxon, an IBM, a General Electric is analogous to losing the embassy of a major power. If that sort of thing proliferates, the country can degenerate into an industrially second-rate nation.

According to one of Italy's major newspaper editors, the basic problem is whether foreign companies are really willing to face the problem of coordinating their goals and actions with those of the social and political actors in the countries where they operate. If not, he says, theories about the multinationals being the only institutions around that can plan a world economy will turn out to be laughably far-fetched:

"If you say, 'we call it quits,' you will have to say the same thing one place after another. To some extent the multinationals have to face the music. The multinationals have the illusion that to some extent—and for an indefinite period—they can avoid having to do this. They believe they can still find countries where the private firm can work in a traditional way. I think this is going to turn out to be largely illusory.

"If I were a prudent manager of a multinational corporation, I would take the easy way out and move back to a place in Europe or elsewhere where the skies are clearer. I would hope they would take the longer view. Italy is an industrial state and Italy is a market. After all, money can be lost elsewhere as easily as in Italy.''

Disinvestment: A Lesser Issue in Canada

Disinvestment, at least to the present moment, has not been a serious issue in Canada. The rate of expansion of U.S. direct investment slowed considerably in the last decade, particularly when compared with the rapid increases in the European Common Market and in other countries like Brazil. But few Canadians seem to see this as a deliberate policy by the United States and, while a few multinational operations have closed down in recent years (often raising some hue and cry), there is no evidence from our interviews that Canadians are preoccupied about a wide pattern of disinvestment.

Yet the situation is clearly volatile. Labor costs in Canada have risen substantially and, in certain sectors, are higher than those in the United States. Indeed, an executive of a U.S.-owned firm in Canada, which has a wage parity agreement across the border, says that the agreement, which served to raise Canadian wages in the past, is now his "sheet anchor in a high wind." Proposed changes in Canadian patent law may well make business conditions extremely difficult for many U.S. firms there.

Finally, recent Canadian policies in a number of areas—foreign investment regulation, natural resources, oil, relations with the Communist nations, the nonpreferential "contractual relationship" with the European Communities, Canada's stand on "national treatment" in the O.E.C.D.—all have contributed to increasing apprehension among American businessmen and government officials.

A senior associate in a major Canadian research organization suggests that American investors are watching the development of the Canadian situation with extreme caution. He says that he believes increasing numbers of U.S. multinationals are adopting a "defensive strategy." He notes: "They stay in Canada only to see if they can outlast their competitors, but with increasingly low profit margins." He suggests further that there has been a spreading belief in business circles in the United States that U.S. investment is now unwelcome in Canada and will be increasingly discriminated against in the future.

Senior managers of a U.S. subsidiary in the pharmaceutical industry underline these opinions. They say U.S. firms in this industry are not expanding, but rather backing out of marginal product lines. The problems in the pharmaceutical industry seem to be the result primarily of recent and proposed changes in regulations affecting the industry, rather than changes in the investment or business climate per se. At the present time, interviews in other industrial areas do not confirm these beliefs. The majority of Americans and Canadians interviewed lead us to believe that there has been no appreciable backlash among U.S. firms to recent Canadian policies—not yet at any rate.

There is another dimension to this matter. We have pointed to a wide consensus in Canada on the utility of the investment review process and on the advocacy of more general efforts to improve the terms of investment in its favor. A leading Canadian business figure cautions, however, that this is a "brittle consensus, and likely to shatter if U.S. firms actually begin to pull out." An adviser to the government similarly asserts that the Canadian government's position quickly collapses when faced by economic adversity. "When push comes to shove," he says, "Canada will still opt for more investment, especially if it promises increased employment."

To this point, the government's position has not been severely tested. The mesh of the screening process has been very wide up to now, and few applications have been rejected. Nor are U.S. firms preparing to take their leave. The situation remains unpredictable.

Part Three
Operational Problems

54

Chapter 7
Patterns of Organization and Management

W E EXPLORED several aspects of this topic with elites in Canada and Italy, and with central and local managers of participating firms. These are among the questions we posed:

(1) How extensive is the use of Americans as top-level managers overseas?

(2) How do local managers who are Canadian or Italian, respectively, feel about career opportunities afforded by the company?

(3) What do managers say about the degree of decisional autonomy available to the affiliate?

(4) What impressions do elites have of the relationship between parent and affiliate?

(5) How do prevailing patterns of decision making impinge on the operations of affiliates?

As was noted in Chapter 3, the question of autonomy has dominated Canadian views. Patterns of decision making within the multinational firm symbolize and underscore for Canadians the high degree of national dependency on the United States. The autonomy of the Canadian affiliate tends to be encompassed in the more basic question of the autonomy of the nation. What we say here about the above questions, and what we say in the concluding chapter about alternative modes of organization, should be judged against this important underlying feeling in Canada.

Local or Expatriate Managers?

Americans in top managerial positions is not an issue in Canada, nor has it been for many years. Fifteen years ago one survey showed that U.S.-controlled companies in Canada overwhelmingly favored using Canadians in technical and professional managerial positions.[1] More recently, Fayerweather concluded that virtually all operating executive positions there have been "Canadianized."[2]

In recent years, more attention has been focused on achieving greater Canadian representations on boards of directors of U.S. subsidiaries. The Business Corporations Act in the province of Ontario was amended in 1973 to require a majority of Canadian residents on boards of directors; a new federal Business Corporations Act, passed in 1975, made this requirement general for all federally chartered

---

[1] John Lindeman and Donald Armstrong, *Policies and Practices of United States Subsidiaries in Canada*. Canada: Private Planning Association of Canada, 1960, pp. 34-5.

[2] John Fayerweather, *Foreign Investment in Canada*. White Plains, New York: International Arts and Sciences Press, Inc., 1973, p. 152.

foreign firms in Canada. Several respondents would go considerably further and require that a certain percentage of board members be Canadians who are not connected with the company.

For a variety of more or less obvious reasons, Europe has been different on this score, and Italy more different than other European countries. From the standpoint of modern management skills, essentially everyone acknowledges that Italy was *tabula rasa* when American firms began to proliferate there in the late 1950's. Indeed, Italians we interviewed are almost of one voice in acknowledging that a key benefit provided by the U.S. firms was the export of modern organization and management technologies.

Even those who criticize the rigid, unadapted application of these methods in Italy recognize this. Indeed, at least half of those in Italy who worry about U.S. firms pulling out emphasize what a serious loss this would be for the continuing training of indigenous managers, and for setting good organization and management standards for other firms.

Nevertheless, Italy today is not what it was twenty years ago. It seems fair to say that many Italians, including indigenous managers of Italian firms, believe that there is excessive use of ''expatriate'' managers in Italy today. Several Italian industrialists, themselves top executives in Italian multinationals, express surprise at the high frequency of American managers in Italy. There is fairly widespread feeling that even where some of the highest managerial positions are opened up to Italians, the very top national position is still not open to them, nor are the key positions in areas like finance. The pattern seems to be that locals are used much more readily in managerial sectors like personnel, marketing, advertising, public and external relations.

Among our participating companies in Canada, all except one chief executive officer are Canadians, although in two cases a Canadian became chief officer for the first time in the corporation only recently. Essentially all of the headquarters managers of these firms are also Canadians. In Italy, on the other hand, three of the seven participating companies had non-Italian chief executives; one was an American and the other two were European.

One of the European managers takes the view that: ''It is natural that the top managers of a corporation should be of the parent nationality.'' He adds that the affiliates of multinationals of his own country are overwhelmingly managed by his countrymen, not by indigenous managers, and he claims that most European multinationals follow the same pattern. The American expatriate manager takes a similar view. He says that when he was at the Harvard Business School he thought that only indigenous persons should manage country affiliates. Now, however, he believes that only expatriates should run overseas multinational company operations. Only those of the parent company's nationality will look at the local situation through the eyes of the parent. Even two to four years of management training outside the foreign country and in the parent company would create only a veneer. ''It would take longer than that to develop the right outlook.'' He recognizes it would be ''demotivating'' for local managers to know that the top jobs are not available, but he would not worry about this. He would apply this principle to all multinationals, not merely American ones.

An American government official in Italy, with extensive direct experience with the industrial community there, agrees with this view. The ideal manager of an affiliate, he believes, is an American who speaks the local language, understands the host country, and can be effective there without taking on the more unattractive aspects of the local business coloration.[3]

Feelings about Career Opportunities

Italian managers in one of these same companies describe it as excessively paternalistic. One in particular indicates that he has, by and large, preferred to work with U.S. companies because they have been much more open and informal than Italian firms. But about the persistence of U.S. managers in Italy, he says:

"We feel we are the hurt and wounded part of Italian management. In an earlier time having expatriates here as managers was a good idea. As we have now developed our own managerial skills, some of those earlier advantages have disappeared. The right philosophy hasn't taken hold. The only advantage is that of having greater confidence in the local manager. But the long hand of the parent is now a bad idea. I insist that we who have been in the company ten, fifteen or more years should have as much of the parent's confidence as do American managers. They sometimes come in here in fact for the subaltern reason of stopping in Italy as birds of passage on their way to brilliant careers with the parent."

Italian managers pretty clearly want to reach top managerial positions of Italian affiliates, as Canadians have recently done. Where this is not possible, they insist that serious morale problems ensue. They are particularly sensitive about the position of CEO. Indeed several of them indicated complete willingness to have the financial management—the "protector of the property and of the stock-holders' interest"—staffed by Americans. In any event, most of our respondents, including nonindigenous managers of Italian affiliates, assume it will be only a matter of time before Italy's managerial situation on this score will be similar to Canada's.

But a number of additional insights emerge from our interviews. For example, Canadians are not completely satisfied with the results of the "Canadianization" of management in U.S. affiliates. They know that many senior positions in these firms are merely paper positions, and that they will have to move south of the border if they wish to keep moving up in the firm. Increasingly, they are unwilling to follow the traditional path southwards to New York or Chicago. Younger managers, in particular, are beginning to demand that the organization create more effective top-level jobs in Canada. Many Canadians deeply resent the formation of "North American" divisions or operations that effectively transfer meaningful positions to the United States.

In the case of smaller U.S. companies, management opportunities within the

---

[3] The characteristics of an ideal affiliate manager are treated also in Burton W. Teague, *Selecting and Orienting Staff for Service Overseas.* The Conference Board, Report No. 705, 1976.

host country are even more limited. Where, in addition, these companies do not evolve a full, integrated development, production and marketing cycle, the mobility opportunities at home are very slim. Thus, either because large-scale American firms in Canada are integrated into U.S. operations, or because the Canadian branches are relatively small, the opportunities for upward movement in Canada are seen as limited and, for that reason, unattractive.

Canadian executives, then, are concerned about whether management jobs there are nothing much more than steps on a career ladder that ends in the United States. Italian executives are concerned that top management may want them to be geographically mobile and might judge their unwillingness to move about as a lack of ambition or of proper orientation to the job. In fact, they tell us that we ought to consider a number of alternative explanations of this reluctance, such as these: first, that to be a top-level manager in a major corporate affiliate in an industrial country like Italy is satisfying enough even for those who have strong appetites for status and material rewards. One Italian CEO notes on this score that his is not only a very high and coveted position in Italy; it is also very high by American managerial criteria.

Second, that Europeans, and particularly Italians, may not find it all that attractive to leave Milan or Rome for most American cities that headquarter the parent firm. One country manager assured us that he gave up a career in the U.S. parent company because neither he nor his wife could survive in the city where it is headquartered. Another noted that not even New York would come close to duplicating the style of life he had come to value. Most of the Italians add that it is simply a mistake to think that the typical European manager wants to reach the very top of a multinational if this implies leaving his own country more or less permanently.

It is worth noting the greater willingness of Italians to consider being posted to regional corporate headquarters located in other major cities of Europe. Indeed, in one of the participating companies, the alleged discrimination in the salaries paid Americans, as opposed to any Europeans holding similar jobs posted to regional headquarters, was said to be a major cause of bad morale throughout the indigenous European managerial group.

Affiliates and Decisional Autonomy

There are some striking Canadian and Italian contrasts and similarities to report here. First, even though Canadians, by and large, desire even greater autonomy for U.S. subsidiaries, there seems in practice to be considerably more of it in Canada than in Italy. This contrast holds true for most of the participating firms in this study.

Second, in both Italy and Canada we find managers pointing to marked differences in the degree of planning and decision-making autonomy available to local affiliates. These differences appear to be related to such factors as:

(1) *The age of the affiliate operation.* How long has a subsidiary existed in a host country; has it sunk roots and does it appear to have taken on the characteris-

tics of a genuine national company? Five of nine participating firms in Canada, and two in Italy, fall into this category. The managers of these affiliates, as well as outsiders who know something about them, make much of these distinctions. In the case of Italy, several managers and elites noted that, until agencies of the U.S. government released sensational information about a number of U.S. multinationals, Italians generally thought of their local affiliates as Italian, not American, firms.

In Canada, several of these firms were already well-established Canadian companies before they were taken over many years ago by a U.S. corporation. Three of the firms participating in our study predate the American parent, and two maintained the original Canadian name for many years.

In most cases these older firms are also those that have used indigenous managers for the longest period. It takes some years—indeed, perhaps a generation—for a firm to develop a pool of indigenous managerial talent from which more senior executives can be selected. During this period, it is far more likely to rely on expatriates.

In Italy, for example, the more knowledgeable Italian elites (such as members of the indistrial community, economists, high-level bureaucrats, non-Italian affiliate managers) expect that as U.S. affiliates currently managed by Americans or Europeans get more experience in Italy they will change over to Italian managerial personnel.

(2) *The equity arrangement.* Many of those we interviewed consider it self-evident that joint ventures provide more local decisional autonomy than do wholly owned subsidiary arrangements. This, of course, is precisely one reason why many U.S. firms are loath to enter into joint ventures. In fact, about one-fourth of the Italians who discuss joint ventures take pains to suggest that creating decisional autonomy because of this factor is not without certain costs. Chief among them would be the possibility that local interest will keep the firm from developing organizational and behavioral standards that go with business modernization and dynamism.

Two respondents, one Italian and one Canadian, each a senior executive in a major multinational corporation headquartered in his own country, provide us with exceptional insights into foreign perceptions of certain aspects of U.S. overseas business. Both are quite pro-American and reluctant to criticize the operations of U.S. multinationals. But both make the same point. They cannot understand, they say, the insistence of U.S. firms on having wholly owned foreign affiliates. The Canadian says, "We would never go abroad without an overseas partner, someone to show us the way." He adds:

"Only through joint ventures can a business get an accurate feeling for the country in which it is dealing and gain the necessary sensitivity to the ways in which business is carried out, to the interests of the country in which it is doing business."

The Italian comments: "Everywhere you Americans go, you arrive with the mentality of Detroit. . . . This is a real error. It creates reactions." He continues:

"Imagine our going to the United Kingdom or to Canada and trying to impose there the Italian way of doing things. . . . When a firm is totally owned by parent companies, it is easier to fall into the trap of rigid dictates to local managers from parent headquarters. Where there is a joint venture, it is easier to get adaptations to local conditions and local norms."

(3) *The scope of local activity.* Our respondents believe that managers of affiliates involved in a full cycle of activity—from planning and research through the development of new products and markets—will be least restrained by regional and central managers. This is obviously going to be even more the case where self-financing arrangements go with the full cycle.

A number of Canadian affiliates fit this pattern. Their managers happily note that the ability of their U.S.-based colleagues to intervene in their decisions is quite limited. In some basic cases they are able to plan and to move ahead with these plans even when Canadian and top management are in disagreement. Managers who enjoy this unusual freedom are quick to add that most U.S. firms in Canada do not fall into this category.

(4) *The corporate function involved.* Corporate respondents at home and abroad tell us that much depends on what is being managed. Labor relations, contacts with governmental agencies, personnel, advertising, adaptation of short-term plans to local situations, tailoring overall policies to fit the laws of a particular country, investment decisions up to a modest and fixed level—these are areas of considerable local direction. Longer term strategies, major investments, product differentiation and specialization, inputs to research, financial arrangements, and development of markets are examples of much more centralized decisions.

One frequent complaint encountered in Canada and Italy is that corporate headquarters often restrict what affiliates can do in the international sphere, or narrowly define how affiliate relationships outside the host country may proceed. Local elites often see these restrictions as evidence that the interests of Canada and Italy are sacrificed in favor of those of the United States. Most of them favor greater pressures on U.S. companies to assure that affiliates will produce for the export market.

On the whole, managers express frustration over restrictions on the scope of their local authority. They say they want more. They add that much of headquarters' talk about local autonomy goes up in smoke at the time of budgetary review, or when financial officers arrive from regional or international headquarters.

(5) *The form of organization.* Managers are of mixed views on this factor. About half of them say that local autonomy is a function not of organizational nuances but, rather, of the abilities and personalities of local managers. Regional managers in particular express this view. One of them in Europe, for example, says that when he was a country director he "fought like hell" to be his own boss, but that now he was doing the same things to "coordinate" company operations under his jurisdiction. "Good Canadian managers," a Canadian tells us, "will fight for more autonomy." An Italian counterpart insists that there is more freedom than meets the eye and that much of what can happen through local

initiative depends on the degree of ingenuity and aggressiveness local management can generate.

Others consider the form of organization to be the critical factor impinging on local autonomy. Several of them cite as examples recent reorganizations in which their own firms were involved. These reorganizations either brought *regional* corporate units into existence or sought to redefine at the regional and parent levels the relationship between area and functional responsibilities.

Local managers point out that the purpose of these reorganizations is to make overall decision making at headquarters more rational and effective. They add, however, that what may appear to be considerable decentralization of responsibility and authority to the regional headquarters becomes, from the vantage point of country operations, much more centralizing in its actual effects.

Centralization at the regional level, we are told, tends to take place by functional category. Functional managers at the country level report in two directions—to the country manager and the regional functional directors—and over time the latter tend to prevail. One of our American respondents in Italy notes that his own firm has two conflicting theories about its recent reorganization. One is that the regional office will exercise relatively light oversight, recognizing that European countries are not comparable to American states. Presumably decisions at the region will be strongly guided and conditioned by country circumstances. In this setting he says, "If a regional man makes plans and policies without interfacing with the locals, he'd be out of his mind. That's how it is now, but it's because our regional people are new and don't know very much."

The other theory he notes is that the marketing managers at regional headquarters will, and should, quickly get to the point where they know what local markets look like and can make the short-term decisions required to run the business. The implication of this is that the region can make decisions for Italy the same way the parent company in the United States makes decisions for Alabama or Oklahoma. He stands deeply opposed to this managerial concept.

An Italian CEO says that whereas the recent reorganization of his company is designed to decentralize, the consequence will be much greater outside control from the region. In an earlier period, his company had a somewhat loose—but nevertheless direct—line to New York. The establishment of the region changes this picture fundamentally. He adds that his prediction grows out of personal experience as a regional functional manager. "Somewhat against my own better judgment, a certain amount of centralization by function tended to occur. The most important countervailing tendency against what top management in New York may want is obviously that of bureaucratization. This happens in part because most of the information the functional manager at the region is digesting is in the form of numbers."

In several of the industrial sectors we looked at, Canada represents a striking exception to the kinds of problems these managers identify. These are cases in which the Canadian subsidiary is considered so important—or has been in existence for such a long time—that Canada is treated as a self-contained *region*. This regional management in Canada comes very close to representing what top managerial organization means in the United States. Canadian managers, as country *and* regional managers, do not have to deal with regional corporate authority whose jurisdiction may encompass widely scattered and diverse local situations in Europe, Latin America, Africa or Asia; nor, in other cases, must they deal with international functional management groups.

From the vantage point of Canadian managers, the next logical step for U.S. firms operating there is to shift from a subsidiary configuration to a major Canadian-based operation with full international responsibilities. Linkage to the parent company in these circumstances would represent a radical transformation of what is now typical of these relationships not only in Canada and Italy, but elsewhere as well.

There is some interesting evidence of international differences on this matter. Studies carried out by Canadian and Italian researchers indicate that there seems to be a difference in patterns of organization and control of European-based and American-based multinationals. Both report that the subsidiaries of American corporations in Canada and Italy tend to be significantly less autonomous than those of European multinationals. The Italian study emphasizes that European multinationals are more willing to enter into joint ventures and even minority equity positions in other countries. The Canadian report suggests that the difference in autonomy seems to be a function of the level at which the Canadian subsidiaries report to the headquarters operation. It claims that, in general, reporting to a European parent occurs at a much higher level. In contrast, the Canadian subsidiary of a U.S. firm is more often seen as one arm of a continental manufacturing and distribution organization.[4]

(6) *The profitability of enterprise.* In the final analysis, though, the managers tell us that the bottom line is a powerful stimulant that greatly affects how much local autonomy is permitted. In the case of one Canadian company, whose local operations resemble not so much a subsidiary as a holding-company unit, a key executive says that economic success, not organizational theories or company ideology, governs local autonomy. This company, he emphasizes, "earned its independence through its continued successful operations."

The other side of this is suggested by an Italian CEO whose local operation has been under very tight rein. The company has been losing large sums of money for several years. He comments:

"Look, the way it goes is that when things are good, when a company is making money, the people in (headquarters city) and (regional city) leave us alone. But, as you can appreciate, when things are going bad in a particular country then, well, (regional city) arrives!"

Canadian and Italian elites believe that these outside controls are exercised much too frequently and insistently. Some of them believe that American com-

   [4] Arthur J. Cordell, *The Multinational Firm, Foreign Direct Investment, and Canadian Science Policy.* Ottawa: Science Council of Canada, 1971, pp. 36-7; and Giorgio Sacerdoti, "Le imprese multinazionali in un mondo di stati," *La communità internazionale,* Vol. 28, 1973, p. 37ff.

panies are in a class by themselves on this score, and some research, referred to above, backs up this belief. A vice president of one of Italy's largest corporations claims that American companies tend toward rigid dictates to local managers, and this entrapment is easiest where the subsidiary is wholly owned and the local managers are Americans. A leader of one of Italy's leading industrial associations comments about the striking lack of elbowroom that characterizes American affiliate managers—Americans or otherwise—in Italy.

Canadian elites are often well aware of the variation in local autonomy that is apparent among U.S. firms operating there. Given the overall Canadian preoccupation with national independence from the United States, it is not surprising that they commend and condemn American firms on this basis.

Italian elites, too, are aware of variations and pay particular attention to U.S. firms that represent greater approximations of the independent national firm. A major U.S. firm is cited as an example of desirable delegation of responsibility to affiliates. The fact that the Italian subsidiary company has worldwide responsibility for certain product lines and that it maintains a major research and development center in Italy is frequently applauded.[5]

Control Patterns and Sensitivity

Overwhelmingly, those who criticize inadequate autonomy for American affiliates believe that this condition leads to insensitivity and failure to adapt to local conditions. Respondents in both countries, and in each elite group, all agreed on this.

Trade union leaders, from whom one might have expected less criticism of this kind given that MNC's normally place the management of personnel and industrial relations in indigenous hands, are as vociferous as any other group. They, too, claim that too much control from the center can lead to much mischief. They too, like local managers and other bureaucrats with whom they must deal, know at firsthand how little real discretion the affiliates have.

But the most telling criticism is from members of the local business community who feel that tight control often impedes intelligent and productive adaptation to local customs. Canadian businessmen, for example, often describe U.S. operations there as overly centralized and insensitive to Canada's needs. Again and again, we found our interviews with Canadian managers began with a ringing denunciation of the Canadian nationalist position, but then concluded with episodes further illustrating the insensitivity to Canada of Americans and U.S. firms.

The charge of insensitivity is not limited to American firms. Italians tell us that managers of English, French, German or other European firms can be as insensitive to local conditions and mores as anyone else. The disastrous outcomes of the Leyland-Innocenti and the Ducati-Thomson crises are chosen as good illustrations of this. Also, American firms are simply more visible, especially in Canada, because there are so many more of them. Yet, as we have seen, Canadians and

---

[5] See *Mondo Economico*, February, 1973, p. 28.

Italians feel that the pattern of organization of U.S. MNC's is significantly more centralized than that of European MNC's. They argue that this centralization encourages the "bulldozer approach of American multinationals."

As noted earlier, snap decisions about disinvestment are said to stem from this organizational problem. Adverse impacts on host-countries' scientific and research development and on export opportunities are also said to result from the inability of U.S. firms to be more aware of and responsive to the interests of the country in which they are operating. The personnel policies of overseas affiliates of U.S. firms are also said to suffer from overcentralization.

Not everyone, however, agrees with these negative views. An economist, with extensive experience in government and industry, says that what strikes one most about U.S. MNC's in Italy and elsewhere in Europe is the extent to which top managers of these firms are captives of their own culture. They do not readily adapt in Italy. His views reflect an image of American managers shared by many Italians, including Italians who manage U.S. firms in Italy, and who are quite loyal to and happy with their own companies. The economist continues:

"On the whole I think this is probably good. Europeans have been taught by American managers that they must do their jobs better, and that they have to do them honestly. Had the Americans been more inclined to adapt, we would not have had this benefit accrue to Italy and Europe."

One might ask, as we sometimes did of respondents, whether insensitivity means lower profits for the firm, or other operating difficulties. Although a few respondents *think* insensitivity hurts profits, they are unable to *show* that this is so. In the case of trade union elites, the answer to the query often is that insensitivity wins the hostility of organized labor—and possibly encourages labor unrest as well. But there is no evidence at all that American companies are targeted by the unions, or that they have demonstrably inferior industrial-relations records in Canada or Italy.

Elites argue instead that raising the question in terms of economic effects may itself be evidence of insensitivity. Rigid emphasis on profits and incremental profit levels is, in their view, part of the problem. They believe that not recognizing this carries profoundly negative long-run implications for the multinational firms. Those implications will also affect profit, but not in the immediate balance-sheet sense that often underlies questions about "sensitivity and so what?"

A Liberal Party MP and industrialist in Italy tells us that Americans must realize that the profit motive as such, and alone, is no longer acceptable in Italy, and that the parent company's isolation from these and other local realities is a prime cause of antagonism toward American business. He is quick to acknowledge the strong points of U.S. MNC's, agrees that they usually outperform Italian companies across the board. But he also wants the American company to persist in Italy. He believes that doing so requires not merely hiring local managers but also providing them with more decisional authority. It requires too, he says, that *international* managers must be more flexible. Above all they must avoid making decisions largely in terms of home-country laws and norms of behavior, or largely in terms of parent-company policies. He concludes: "To adapt is not merely a matter of respecting local laws. It is also a matter of participating in local culture."

The chief economist of a major Italian firm says:

"When profit levels are not up to what one has projected at the center, managers arrive from headquarters and say change what you are doing—or else. The troops arrive when things go badly. The violent modes of intervention from New York, exporting your American tendency to have high levels of managerial turnover, are fundamentally unnatural to Italian corporate enterprise. In Italy we just don't change high and middle managers as often as you do. Anyway, Italy has little experience with this kind of centralized control."

On balance, respondents seem to be saying that, even though American firms abroad are often spectacularly successful on the economic side, they could be better integrated in host countries without jeopardizing profits. In fact, as we will show later, there are many who believe that better integration would produce more politically relevant data that will deeply affect the long-term future of these firms.

One of our more perceptive respondents draws an analogy from the Roman Empire:

"The Romans had a rule that whoever is part of an organization outside Rome also becomes a civic person there. By way of contrast the multinationals represent the opposite of this; they show a lack of integration into Italian society. The real enemies of the multinationals are located inside the companies. Because they are always proconsuls and never full-fledged citizens."

In the end, we cannot *prove* that greater sensitivity to host-country environments is a necessary condition for successful industrial and commercial activity abroad. We recognize not only that there are distinct differences of opinion between parent and affiliate managers over how much sensitivity (and, by implication, local discretion) should prevail, but also that, by any test, American companies vary considerably among themselves.

Furthermore, we are aware that individual companies, as multinationals, differ as to whether they should be sensitive to these matters at all. When interests collide, most would agree that those of the parent prevail over those of the subsidiary. Some parent headquarters utilize a degree of insensitivity to host countries as a means of maintaining distance from the affiliates, and as a means of encouraging more aggressive competition among affiliates for allocations from the center.

We *can* say without question that the overriding criticisms local elites make of U.S. firms operating in their countries turns on the insensitivity issue. This is their major perception; alongside it, talk about codes of conduct and the social responsibility of the multinational enterprise seems to them hollow and disingenuous. They state flatly that insensitivity and *bad* corporate citizenship are not only tied together, they often amount to one and the same thing.

These elites are opinion leaders. They are influential. Often they say and do things that greatly affect the future of enterprise. In short, what they think and believe counts, it can—and probably will—make a difference. At least the local managers of U.S. firms operating in Canada and Italy think so.[6]

---

[6] See Michael G. Duerr and John M. Roach, *Organization and Control of International Operations,* The Conference Board, Report No. 597, 1973, for a wide survey of the international organization of North American, European and Japanese multinationals; see also James R. Basche, Jr., *Integrating Foreign Subsidiaries in Host Countries,* The Conference Board, Report No. 506, 1970.

Chapter 8
Labor and Industrial Relations

LABOR and industrial relations, in the strict sense, are not a basis for criticisms of multinationals, either in Canada or in Italy. If anything, the U.S. companies are considered to be exemplars in this area. Trade union leaders in both countries, administrative officials who are close to practices of labor and industrial relations, economists, intellectuals, mass media leaders, and political party officials are essentially of one view on this score. American firms normally display a pattern of strict, scrupulous adherence to local laws and regulations. It is noteworthy that labor relations is not a topic discussed by the several official Canadian reports on problems created by the multinational corporation.

Our findings in Italy are consistent with what the International Labour Organization has found to be the case elsewhere in Western Europe. A recent report of that organization, encompassing six countries, concludes that the multinationals have a very good record of adapting to local laws and practices pertaining to industrial relations. Where there are deviations—for example on the matter of union recognition—they seem to stem from the degree of strictness about such matters that exists in host countries. In any case, the ILO finds that multinational practices are not different from those of local firms.[1]

Canada and the "International" Unions

Canadian labor leaders spend a good deal of time discussing their relations with the "international" unions, and they are aroused by their perceived organizational dependence within these unions. It must be noted that "international union" in this context refers to North American unions that organize both Canadian and American workers and are usually headquartered in the United States.[2] Many Canadian trade unionists believe that the same relationship that prevails between Canada and the United States in business and industry is reproduced within the trade unions.

Canadian trade union leaders, therefore, have sought greater autonomy of their own. They have also maintained an independent voice and posture within the ILO

[1] International Labour Organization, *Multinationals in Western Europe: The Industrial Relations Experience*. Geneva, 1976. For employer, worker and government representatives' reactions to this and three other ILO reports, see ILO, *Tripartite Advisory Meeting on the Relationship of Multinational Enterprise and Social Policy, Report of Meeting, May 4-12, 1976*. Geneva, 1976. See as well, ILO, *Social and Labor Practices of Some European-Based Multinationals in the Metal Trades*. Geneva: ILO, 1975; ILO, *Wages and Working Conditions in Multinational Enterprises*. Geneva: ILO, 1976. The last study has been much criticized because of the extremely fragmentary nature of the statistical data.

[2] See John Crispo, *International Unionism: a Study in Canadian-American Relations*. Toronto: McGraw Hill Company of Canada, 1967. In the book, Crispo suggests that Canadian branches of the unions do, in fact, have a significant degree of autonomy.

and the ICFTU. Within that international context, the Canadian unions have played an important role in trying to define what should be the role and responsibilities of the MNC's in Third World countries.

At home, however, Canadian unions have not been major critics of the multinationals. There are occasions when labor disputes may lead to a certain amount of rhetoric about multinationals, but these cases are felt to be rare. More often than not, Canada's labor leaders claim that, in the sphere of industrial relations, U.S. firms operating there are at least as good corporate citizens as Canadian-owned firms—and frequently better.

Canadian labor demands, we are told, differ little from those in the United States. In one participating firm, which carries on simultaneous labor negotiations on both sides of the border, Canadian agreements differ from American "largely in the area of fringe benefits which are due to different governmental social welfare policies and to different in-plant arrangements." These in-plant differences seem to focus mainly on mandatory overtime, which Canadians resist more vigorously than Americans. A senior manager in charge of labor relations in one firm in the project observes that Canadian workers' views on workers' control or participation are the same as Americans'—"they want no part of these arrangements." [3]

Canadians tell us that this union posture is entirely in keeping with the political conservatism that has characterized the trade unions of that country. It was evidently the trade union segment within the New Democratic Party that helped in 1972 to defeat the "Waffle Group," a left faction with very aggressive attitudes toward foreign capital and MNC's in Canada. In Canada, leaders are becoming aware of growing complaints by American unions that the U.S. multinationals are exporting jobs to other countries. Some Canadians feel that this tends to dampen what might otherwise be more biting criticisms from the trade union sector.

Canadian and Italian trade union leaders are much *less* inclined than other elites to place American multinationals in a separate category, or to suggest that the problem of the multinationals is essentially limited to the United States. An Italian labor leader takes pains to say that when it comes to the insensitivity of local managers to the nuances associated with labor practices, American company managers are no better or worse than those of other multinationals. In Italy it was a *banker,* not a labor leader, who said: "The emblem of the multinational corporation is the emblem of the United States. These two concepts are fundamentally indistinguishable." Most Italian labor leaders agree in effect with the Canadian official who remarks that the nationality of a parent company is immeasurably less important than the fact of foreign ownership itself insofar as labor relations are concerned.

Italy and the Political Role of Unions

In their political, rather than their industrial roles, however, trade union elites are among the most vociferous critics of the multinationals. Canadian unions

---

[3] The "workers' participation" movement is not very well advanced in Italy either. However, one reason for this is that major trade-union leaders there consider most forms of it quite useless.

within the New Democratic Party are articulate and outspoken Canadian nationalists, and have pressed for greater Canadian national independence. Italian trade union leaders have led the public attack on those multinationals in Italy that try to reduce their labor forces or go out of business. It is typically the last stage of the disinvestment drama that union-led workers occupy the plant just before one public agency or another steps in to absorb the failed or abandoned industrial enterprise.

Given the highly politicized role trade unions play in Italy, against the background of rising labor costs and the Workers' Law of 1969, it is natural that there should be attacks on MNC's on broader ideological grounds. For example, four of Italy's foremost labor leaders—two of them Communists, two Christian Democrats—score American multinationals in particular for not coming to terms with the new system of industrial relations ushered in by the Workers' Law. They add that American firms are particularly adept at undercutting union efforts to introduce workers' councils and other forms of participation in the plant. One trade unionist claims: "There is often a conceptual refusal by Americans to accept industrial relations as they exist here. You must remember that since 1969 the employers of this country have been tied to new and fundamentally unprecedented regulations regarding their institutional role in society. It has not been easy for them to recognize this reality and to make an equilibrated adaptation to it."

An Italian banker tends to agree. He suggests that Italy has been leading what may be a widespread, revolutionary change in industrial relations policy that may spread to all of Europe. It is not just a matter of high labor costs but a new philosophy of industrial enterprise. It goes beyond self-management and relates fundamentally to the question of whether labor is governable on the bases of traditional institutions and mechanisms. Indeed, he adds, the basic question is whether, given the changed attitudes of Italians toward work itself, the Communist Party is capable of facing a showdown with the unions.

One major Communist leader comes at this matter somewhat differently. American and other foreign companies in Italy must come around to the realization that they cannot cope with problems of the firm by laying off or firing workers. The new concept of industrial relations will not permit this. On the other hand, he says the Communist Party is aware that absenteeism is out of hand, that productivity is dropping, that it is next to impossible to fire a worker anymore, and that these are prime factors that cause multinationals to wonder about reinvesting or disinvesting. He adds that the Communist Party is working on plans to deal with this problem.

Although many of Italy's elites recognize that the 1969 Workers' Law, as interpreted by the courts, is a prime cause of high labor costs, union leaders are less inclined to acknowledge this. They tend to agree with one of the Law's authors, who claims that the real reason employers in Italy—national and multinational alike—are angry is that the old system of industrial relations is gone. In any case, labor leaders are loath to accept new negotiations on such critical issues as sick leaves, absenteeism or double employment (an Italian practice that admittedly hits the MNC doubly hard). Nevertheless, several of them acknowledge that those in

Italy who say that the Workers' Law has become an explosive political weapon are correct.[4]

Because the Italian trade unions have been radicalized, because they are located in Europe and not in North America, they are more prone to stress that national governments and national unions are inadequate to cope with the problems created by multinationals. Italian labor leaders are among the foremost in Europe in pressing for common strategies that will reduce the maneuverability of multinationals in labor negotiations and conflict. They say they wish to promote a code of conduct by the European Communities, and standard legislation for dealing with MNC's by each national government in Europe. They support cross-national collective bargaining work stoppages in every country in which an affiliate of a given multinational may be located.[5]

Above all, the Italians are trying to strengthen the European Confederation of Trade Unions. They agree absolutely with other Europeans who hold that just as the unions, in the last century, had to become national as the firm became national, so they will have to follow the firm again, and become multinational.[6]

At a mid-1976 London meeting, Italian trade union leaders put forward a platform and operational code. They are not sanguine that it will be implemented concretely in the short run. Indeed, most of them identify the working class in Europe, and its union representatives, as highly parochial and potentially very nationalistic.

Some of them, interestingly enough, fear that the multinational enterprise may turn out to be devastatingly effective in encouraging "plant-level nationalism." Because the multinationals tend to have more enlightened managers than is true locally; because they do not cut corners on basic industrial relations laws; because they build safe, modern, clean plants with worker amenities; and because they often lead as well in wage policies—these are reasons, they say, why the multinational may destroy labor solidarity and cause workers in these plants to break off from the rest of the trade union movement.[7]

Some of the Canadian and Italian firms participating in the study are not unionized. One of these firms maintains a nonunion plant in an Italian city that has voted overwhelmingly Communist in every election since 1946. In the past, the Communist-dominated union attempted to unionize the plant without success. Local managers explain this by the company's excellent wage policy, its willingness to permit its workers to go out on strike during national contract negotiations,

---

[4] This problem is discussed at length by Tiziano Treu (ed.), *L'uso politico dello Statuto dei lavoratori*. Bologna: Il Mulino, 1975.

[5] See, ILO, *Tripartite Advisory Meeting, op. cit.*, pp. 8-9, for some interesting labor representative comments on the transnational labor movement.

[6] See the important publication, *Syndicats et sociétés multinationales*. Paris: La Documentation Française, 1975.

[7] For a somewhat polemical but interesting discussion of this point, see Angelo Genari, "La presenza delle imprese multinazionali in Italia nei diversi settori produttivi," *Quaderni di azione sociale*, No. 4/6, 1973, p. 41ff.

and its overall plant record for hygiene, safety and other amenities. By and large, the company has been left pretty much alone.

Other nonunionized firms in our study have had similar experiences. The fact that they are not unionized is noted by respondents, but labor leaders do not make a major point of this. On the whole, elites in both countries seem to think that the question of nonunionization is not particularly germane, and certainly not restricted to multinational enterprises.

One or two Canadians suggest that this may prove troublesome down the road. Six or seven Italians believe that, as the country moves left politically, nonunion plants will have to come around. No one makes this prediction with much confidence.

These Italian union concerns, and efforts to cope with them, do not pertain exclusively to American firms. They are obviously part of a Europeanwide movement in which Canada is also involved, and in which Italian trade union leaders tell us they hope the American unions will become involved as well. For further comment on this, see Chapter. 13.

Chapter 9
Governmental Relations and Political Analysis

ENTERING a foreign country as a direct investor is a complex technical and political process about which much has been written. Multinational firms husband or hire highly skilled legal, financial and other technical and professional experts to cope with the entry problem. Entering itself brings corporate managers and representatives into direct contact with the public bureaucracy, the legal institutions, and the business community of the host country. The local U.S. diplomatic community will also often be involved. Inevitably, one or more federal agencies in the United States will take notice of and also influence these investment ventures.

There is little to add to what others have reported about this process.[1] Our attention was concentrated on two dimensions of corporate organization that become important *after* the affiliate has become operational abroad. First, we explored the kinds of relationships that affiliates establish within the political sphere, broadly conceived, and with agencies of the host-country government. Second, we wished to assess whether, to what extent, and how American firms operating overseas include political analysis in their decision making regarding affiliates.

Relations with Host Governments

In both Canada and Italy, U.S. firms try to maintain a low profile if they can, and prefer to avoid direct contacts with political parties and governmental authorities. This may be surprising for some, for there are studies of Canada that suggest that the business community is quite prominent in national decision making.[2] In general, our Canadian respondents do not agree.

The Italian findings, however, are entirely consistent with the generally well-known tendency of the Italian industrial community to steer clear of open involvement in politics.[3] Indeed, the refusal of Italian industrialists to be more visibly committed politically became a major issue within the General Confederation of Italian Industry a few years ago. Two of our respondents were intimately involved in an effort by younger industrialists and MP's to change that posture.[4]

---

[1] See, for example, the recent study by Jack N. Behrman, J.J. Boddewyn, and Ashok Kapoor, *International Business-Government Communications.* Lexington, Mass.: Lexington Books, 1975.

[2] See R. Presthus, *Elite Accommodation in Canadian Politics.* Cambridge: The University Press, 1973, pp. 176-177, 206-207. The author is careful to hedge what he has to say about the relative influence of business, labor and other groups. Another view of the political effectiveness of Canadian business is provided by J.A. Murray and M.C. Gerace, "Multinational Business and Canadian Government Affairs," *Queen's Quarterly,* Vol. 80, Summer, 1973, pp. 222-232.

[3] See J. LaPalombara, *Interest Groups in Italian Politics.* Princeton: Princeton University Press, 1963.

[4] This important report is available from the Confindustria. Comitato Centrale dei Gruppi Giovani Industriali, *Una politica per l'industria.* Rome: Confederazione Generale dell'Industria Italiana, 1969.

They report that the Italian businessman's loathing for political parties and politicians—his fear of defending the business position in public, and his inability to develop coordinated politically relevant activity in his own self-interest—runs very deep.

Many of the political party and mass media elites among our Italian respondents prefer that industrial managers not be politically active. They express alarm that in 1976 even one of them, Umberto Agnelli, should have become a candidate for Parliament, openly espousing the cause of the private sector. Taken all together, these attitudes amount to saying that it is legitimate for all organized groups—*except* the business community—to pursue their interests through political instrumentalities. Often the same respondents who say they would prefer that business not be *openly* involved politically complain the loudest about *covert* political intervention by the industrial community.

Canadian respondents, including government officials, express some surprise at the relatively minor political role U.S. firms play in Canada. They feel that the managers of U.S. firms prefer to opt out, and that affiliates with American rather than Canadian managers opt out more than others. A Canadian comments that the frequent movement of affiliate managers in and out of Canada tends to limit their effectiveness in developing and utilizing contacts with government.

These views differ somewhat from the Gray Report finding that the "United States corporate view" has an important voice in the Canadian political arena. The report itself, however, lays out no evidence that the behavior of American-owned firms differs in any significant way from that of Canadian firms in Canadian elections.[5]

One of Canada's provincial cabinet ministers notes that in his experience U.S. firms have never attempted blatantly to influence policy through bribes or payoffs. Rather, he expresses surprise that there has not been more of an effort to cultivate regularized relationships with the government. Some of the same view is expressed in Italy, although recent scandals about political contributions—open or covert, legal or illegal—lead several of our respondents to underscore that they are opposed to the use of money to exert political pressures, or to elicit political favors. In Canada and in Italy there are many persons (often high-level bureaucrats, ministers, deputy ministers, and MP's) who feel that things might be better all around if multinationals were more directly present in the decision-making process. One of Canada's most deeply committed nationalists expresses no concern at all about the political rectitude and probity of affiliate managers of U.S. firms. They are, he says, "the best-behaved foreign capitalists in the world."

An Italian MP and industrialist believes that more active and conscious political involvement is a necessary condition for successful operations in his country:

"One knows that, in a country like Italy, business and politics are so intertwined one cannot do without politics. Yet American firms shun this; they fear getting into the political sphere. This creates a completely distorted conception within these firms of what is going on in Italy, what Italy is."

[5] See *Foreign Direct Investment in Canada*. Ottawa: Government of Canada, 1972, pp. 301-306.

73

Not many respondents believe that business managers are going to become more directly involved politically than in the past. In both Canada and Italy the businessman's reluctance to do this is more than matched by those who (for various and often quite different reasons) believe that the relationship between the public and private sector should remain highly separate and distinct.

To shun direct political involvement does not also imply that business will be able to avoid relating to agencies of governments. Both in Canada and in Italy there are American firms that by reason of what they produce and sell must maintain regularized ongoing relations with national and regional public administrative bodies. Often top-level legislative and executive officials become involved as well. Industrial firms in the energy, electronics, aerospace and related fields cannot do without government contacts for many reasons. Where the products involved are considered to affect public health, or where the government as a matter of policy controls and administers prices, regularized contacts with public agencies are built-in and required. Where acquiring tariff protections or other concessions from government is a necessary condition for continuing in business, contacts with government are also to be expected.

This does not mean that affiliate managers will be comfortable about their contacts. In Italy, for example, managers of U.S. affiliates in the above categories identify having to deal with the Italian bureaucracy as their number-one operating problem. The problem does not center on the technical competence of Italy's administrators; in complex fields like petroleum, pharmaceuticals, food and chemical products, U.S. affiliate managers tell us that administrative officials are often highly competent. Even those managers (a minority) who feel that bureaucrats lack technical competence add that the latter can be taught to understand the complexities of particular industrial problems.

The problem in Italy is more often politics. Ministers who know that petroleum companies are losing money refuse for months to recommend or to grant price increases, because they fear political repercussions from political leaders and the mass media. Mass media and left-wing party leaders readily agree that, at least in recent years, all petroleum companies in Italy have been losing money. Publicly, however, they take stands against price rises, and attack ministers and high-level bureaucrats who grant them.

Politics also deeply affects the operations of pharmaceutical companies. Italian respondents who know that this industry has considerable transfer pricing agree with affiliate managers who say they cannot do otherwise in a country where patents for pharmaceutical products do not exist, and where small firms are certain to pirate new products in a few short years. The same chief editor whose paper has often and frequently attacked U.S. companies in this sector acknowledges that many of the questionable multinational practices there are encouraged by existing Italian policies. A leading Communist MP agrees with him. "Before we can hope to discipline the multinationals," he says, "we will have to put our bureaucratic house in order."

There is another side to this story as well. High-level bureaucrats, ministers, economic experts who have dealt with multinational representatives note that candor has not been their most striking quality. Where American firms are known to have distorted their reports on operations in the past, Italian decision makers will view them with suspicion long after the firm itself may have developed more acceptable standards of disclosure. Thus, one petroleum executive says he lives in a "glass house" but despairs that Italian bureaucrats, politicians and journalists do not believe what they see there. The composite reply to this seems to be that the glass house is of very recent construction and that here and there the glass still seems quite opaque.

Many Italians, including several affiliate managers, agree that the multinational firm lacks credibility today. With rare exception the greatest skepticism is expressed by administrators who deal with MNC affairs. Some of this results from convincing evidence that particular firms have hidden or distorted the truth; some results from highly publicized and sensationalized cases of wrongdoing that may involve a handful of firms but affect all multinationals as a category. Some of it, Italians acknowledge, also stems from deliberate campaigns to use any means— including the telling of falsehoods and the spreading of rumor—to place the multinationals in the worst possible light.

We must add here the laconic observation of an Italian newspaper managing director and person with extensive experience with a wide range of Italian elites: "When the multinational is attacked, there isn't anyone in Italy who will step forward to defend it." This view is reflected in the account of an Italian chief executive officer of a large American firm. Some time ago, he had seen a friend of his among demonstrators who were passing in front of the firm's headquarters on their way to hold a public rally that had nothing to do with his company. Nevertheless, someone tossed a Molotov cocktail through the front door. He later reported this to his friend and asked for an explanation. His friend replied, "Look, it is never really a bad thing to throw a Molotov cocktail at an American multinational."

It is essential to record that respondents do not believe that multinational firms are singled out for discriminatory treatment in Canada or Italy. On the contrary, affiliate managers in Italy assure us that behavior is not only even-handed, but that often men and women in the ministries will go to some pains to deliver unusually privileged treatment.

The problem in Italy is that multinational affiliates are treated to the same combination of factors that strike many of these managers as sheer madness, and therefore exceptional, whereas Italians know this behavior, however insane, is normal and routine. Thus a European who manages one of our participating company affiliates in Italy expresses his astonishment over discovering that, regarding administered prices for his industry, "every single step along the way is politicized in Italy." He adds:

"The problem is not that prices are administered; the system is really well thought out. It is that the same rules Italians themselves develop are either not applied, or cannot be applied except on the basis of politics.

"This damn bureaucracy strangles everything. It is really a horrendous thing.

As a (nationality), I can tell you it's unheard of in my country. In spite of this, though, we do very well. How do we manage? Because we are slim and lean here.''

The Canadian situation differs markedly from what we find in Italy. Managers report few day-to-day problems in dealing with administrative agencies there. On the one side, as a manager in an American-owned firm in Canada observes: ''In Canada, U.S. subsidiaries know what the law is and are not subject to constant change and to bureaucratic uncertainties or instabilities.''

On the other side, bureaucrats in the Canadian government acknowledge that U.S. subsidiaries are almost always straightforward and aboveboard in their dealings with the government. In Canada the public administration is held in high regard. This is unlike Italy, where it is the object of almost universal disdain. U.S. subsidiaries follow national patterns.

There is some evidence that the Canadian situation may be changing. Several Canadian business leaders and managers of U.S. firms in Canada express alarm at the ''spreading socialism'' of the Trudeau government. (One refers to it as ''communism.'') There is substantial business opposition in Canada to recent government policies in a number of sectors. The Prime Minister's 1975 Christmas message certainly calmed none of these concerns. But there is a clear distinction made between the content or direction of government policy and its administration. Even with the application of price and wage controls (initiated in 1975), Canadians do not see the public administration itself as an unusual source of frustrations.

Where some difficulties do occur, we are told that they often involve affiliates getting caught up in tensions between federal and provincial authorities. For example, relations between these two levels are in such flux regarding the control of natural resources that some complicating spillover is inevitable for managers of affiliates in the extractive sector.

Federalism also carries certain inconveniences in a firm's relations with government that occur less often where there is greater centralization of national policy and administration. In Italy, for example, pharmaceutical companies deal essentially with one or two national ministries, however frustrating these contacts may be. In Canada, on the other hand, the affiliates of the same American companies have to deal with as many as eleven different governments (one national, ten provincial), each of which has different requirements affecting this industry. However, as the powers of Italian regional governments expand, and a form of de facto federalism emerges, similar problems will confront American firms operating there.

In their relationships with governments, American firms in Italy and Canada do not encounter much difficulty regarding information disclosure. Both countries have deeply rooted liberal traditions that govern business dealings with the government. Governments in both countries go to great pains to respect business confidentiality; neither country comes close to extracting from industrial firms the types of information that U.S. state and national governments elicit and get as a matter of course. Indeed, by Italian standards the amount of information that most American affiliates willingly make public there is a source of frequent praise—as well as amazement—among those we interviewed.

Our respondents tell us there are serious costs that grow out of the tendency to shun politics, and to keep relations with administrative agencies at the minimum necessary for operations. Among these, the most important is said to be that neither affiliate nor parent will learn to make informed, sophisticated judgments about the political factors that can and do influence a company's well-being. A Canadian respondent comes down hard on this point: He believes that the potential in political learning is worth all the hassles that greater political and administrative involvement on the part of the multinational firm might imply.

Political Analysis

This raises the issue of whether American firms use politically relevant information in their decision making, where they go to get such information, and how such information is integrated and weighed along with other factors that govern corporate decisions at home or in the field. With one or two exceptions, the answer in Canada and Italy seems to be "no" on all counts.

One source for multinationals wishing to gather political information about particular foreign countries might be the United States government, at home or overseas. But such requests for information are quite rare. Moreover, it is not clear that the Administration could be genuinely helpful if there were more such requests.

In Washington

Our initial interviews in Washington suggested that as a routine matter relatively few requests for information reach country specialists in the Department of State. One of these specialists, an expert in economic affairs, suggests that the only time an American firm asks for his attention is when the company is already in real trouble overseas. Occasionally a company may call to ask for an interpretation of an election or of a particular political event, but these occurences are relatively rare.

One impression expressed in Washington is that American companies have their own independent ways of getting the "political low-down" on what is going on abroad. By comparison, the embassies overseas do not regularly transmit information to Washington regarding what may sweeten or poison the business climate in a host country. Parent companies, this official believes, are much more likely to rely on the political reporting provided by their own affiliates in those countries.

As country situations become more problematical and perplexing, the number of inquiries to Washington seems to rise as well. For example, political contributions that created furors that involved Canada and Italy led to more telephone and direct inquiries from U.S. firms with operations in these countries. Similarly, as Canadians nationalize a basic resource like potash and begin wondering how to treat other extractive industries, more inquiries are directed to Washington. In the Canadian case, however, there seems to be the assumption—often infuriating to

Canadians—that Canada is essentially like the United States and Americans know a good deal of what is transpiring there politically.

It may be true, our respondents suggest, that some of the largest U.S. corporations do systematically gather and use politically relevant data from Canada. Certainly two of our participating firms in that country reveal a great deal of contact between local managers and the Canadian government, and careful as well as sophisticated analysis of political and social trends. It is instructive that the managers of one of these firms say that such information is largely for their own use and is not requested by the parent company in the United States.

In any case, the larger American firms that consciously try to include political analyses in their decision making are the exception. We are told that even there we should be careful not to overestimate how much energy, conscious planning, and sophisticated analysis may actually go into this process.

In the case of most other American companies operating abroad, what one U.S. official says about our neighbor to the north would apply to Italy too:

"Most of the questions I get from American industries reveal an appalling lack of information about Canada. When they do call, they generally have no idea whatever of how I might be useful to them or what I might be able to tell them. Their questions aren't very pointed."

Overseas

The situation is not markedly different in the field. Embassy officials, consular officers, and affiliate managers tell us that they rarely if ever have any contact with each other. In Canada, where such a high proportion of affiliate managers are Canadians, it is described as unlikely that these persons would approach U.S. diplomatic officials for political information or analysis about their own country. Italian managers respond similarly; where they manage U.S. corporations, they feel they have relatively little need to turn to the U.S. Embassy for information about Italy.

A second factor operating here is the penchant for low profile and the antipathy toward politics and politicians noted earlier. Affiliate managers whose firms are not necessarily or widely identified as American say they try to avoid contacts and associations that would change that. In one important Italian case, in fact, the managing director's prime reason for *not* wanting to publish a "code of conduct" prepared by the parent company is the risk that his so far "invisible" company will surface as a U.S. multinational.

Neither in Canada nor in Italy, then, do American business managers maintain regular contacts with, or solicit politically relevant information from U.S. diplomatic officials. Some of the latter who were interviewed for this study feel that political information is not solicited because corporate officials do not know what to do with it; others suggest that political factors are treated as random because corporate officers feel they cannot control them. One foreign service officer says that often it is the U.S. affiliate (or parent) that provides the U.S. embassy with information because they have more of it than the government does.

How do the affiliate managers feel about all of this? First, they suggest that there may be some truth to the idea that corporate managers know more than foreign service officers about specialized aspects of politics and administration abroad. This belief is based on the direct experience of several American managers interviewed.

Second, where U.S. affiliates abroad are managed by Americans, they tend to place locals in charge of external and governmental relations. Where legal services or interventions with administrative agencies are required and unavailable through the affiliate itself, they are usually purchased. However, the managers acknowledge that buying such services on the local market is not without cost, risk and, sometimes, painful surprises.

Third, managers say that they, or at least other managers of the affiliate, are likely to be around in a given country longer than the typical foreign service officer who passes through on a two- or four-year tour. Younger officers in particular, they believe, have little to tell them. Fourth, the affiliate managers interviewed deeply believe that not nearly enough attention is paid by their organizations, particularly at headquarters, to the need for producing good political intelligence and analysis.

The Use of Political Analysis by U.S. MNC's

One Canadian president of a participating firm notes that little or no political forecasting goes into the company's long-term planning, nor is there any conscious attention to the political aspects of key assumptions even for short-term planning. He anticipates that political assessments will increase in the future.

Another Canadian affiliate manager says that, until the Gray Report appeared, he believed that his company was engaged in quite sophisticated political analysis—at least locally. They have since changed their minds and expanded their external relations capacity, both internally and through the use of outside consultants. Nevertheless, he adds that it has never been easy to convince senior managers of the corporation of the need for this kind of analysis inside or outside the company.

The manager of the corporate planning department of another U.S. affiliate in Canada says that political variables are treated informally. The firm has never been very good at incorporating social and political dimensions into its long-term planning. Planning proceeds on the assumption that the political situation will remain stable.

In Italy, a U.S. government official claims it is precisely this lack of attention to careful political analysis that leads to panicky precipitous corporate decisions there. The CEO of an American company there says that industrialists should not shun politics, but rather should become "political men" and gain a better understanding of the political process.

Over a dozen managers of U.S. affiliates in Italy, as well as some indigenous elites and members of the U.S. diplomatic community, commented on the issue of whether—and how—political information and analysis is used in corporate decision making. On the whole, the managers tell us that very little attention is paid to this matter. One of the largest corporations in the world, according to one of its top officials, handles political reporting strictly as general background, and adds perhaps a few footnotes to the annual report from Italy which is essentially an economic document. A second affiliate manager reports the same pattern; some political "backgrounding" goes into quarterly and annual *economic* reports that go from the affiliate to the parent office.

An American managing director says: "I would say we have one report, written by our financial man, who comments on social, political and economic developments here. It won't tell you more than you would get reading the newspapers in New York. On the other hand, short of making a deal with the CIA, I don't see what we could do to help [headquarters] understand what's going on here."

A second impression our respondents create is that parent companies do not really value political reporting. Reports often go to financial officers in the parent's offices; these are said not to care at all about political factors unless it can be clearly shown how they relate to the company's financial condition. The low interest in this kind of information is also said to be mirrored in the fact that it is generally produced by public affairs or a similar division of the multinational.

A third impression is that political analyses of a more than superficial and impressionistic kind tend to be concentrated at times of entering or bailing out of a given country. In between these two critical points most firms evidently consider political inputs to be, at best, marginal to their decisions. It is this that leads one Italian to assert that the American multinationals are notoriously badly informed about local political factors. It is perhaps this, too, that underlies an American managing director's surmise that: "They don't give a damn about these reports. It's not clear that they are ever read."

A fourth impression is that not enough serious attention has been paid to the possible utility of incorporating political analysis into decision making and giving it status somewhat closer to the kind of economic analysis central directors demand. One CEO of an overseas affiliate tells us, for example, that he was surprised and then pleased to note in our format of interview topics that we wished to include a discussion of political analysis. He surmises that, while it is possible to get corporate officials to read these reports, managers at London or Paris, New York, Philadelphia, Pittsburgh or Houston are not prepared to evaluate this kind of information. Why?

"Because of the 'numbers and tables mentality' that has taken hold of the corporation. At a certain level of management the company can't make a decision until there is that mound of tables before us to stare at. I want to say, 'Turn off the lights, let's sit here for a few hours, do some thinking, and see what we come up with.' The most important kind of information I can provide for them is this political type. This is also the type they will least frequently request."

A managing director of another affiliate says our questions about political analysis jolted him. "There isn't any request at all from [headquarters] for what you call political intelligence." He adds:

"If I were at headquarters I would want exactly this type of information. This is the kind of information that would be terribly useful to the people at (headquarters). I hadn't thought about the fact that we could play a role in getting it."

Few senior executives in the headquarters of U.S. MNC's seem really to underline the need for sophisticated political analysis of this type. The views expressed by one, the CEO and chairman of the board of a major multinational, and a European, are very atypical:

"The most important weapon I have, and I get it from my country managers, is on the political side. This is basic. It is more important than any of the economic information they send. I tell you I get better information in the countries where we are operating than the Italian government does. This is far and away the best weapon around. I consider it a formidable weapon."

Two officials of the Federal Government provide sobering and, perhaps, helpful reflections. One of them, in Washington, believes that an earlier reluctance of American executives to become directly involved in the administrative and political process may be changing. American business, he says, has been ill-equipped to intervene in the political process, often relying on heavy-handed, cigar-chewing lobbyists who are no longer any match for those who staff legislative committees and the bureaucracy.

"Businessmen are trained to produce widgets," he says. "They do not understand the subtleties of the political process. They are also poorly informed about policies and policy proposals that affect their interests. This is true except for a handful of the largest MNC's. They believe that PR—like good corporate deeds—will produce benign conditions here and abroad." He feels, however, that events of recent years are sending more CEO's to Washington than ever before.

In Rome, another U.S. official sums up his beliefs about political participation and analysis by U.S. multinationals:

"For a good long time in a country like Italy (but in other countries, too) American businesses did not have to worry about such things. The economy was booming, the Italian government was happy to have the investment, jobs were being maintained or added to, profits were being returned for both the local market and for the multinational stockholders. Now that things have taken a turn for the worse—and I believe they are going to continue that way for some time, even if the world economic situation turns around—corporate managers are becoming more interested in political factors. Now businesses have to worry about government policies and have to worry more than they ever have before about what those policies may mean for their own survival."

Chapter 10
Codes of Conduct

OUR RESPONDENTS are of strikingly varied opinions about "codes of conduct" designed to guide or restrict corporate behavior. As a group they are also reasonably well informed that individual corporations, national governments, and international organizations have either enacted such codes or are actively considering doing so.

A very early example of efforts at national regulation of corporate behavior took place in Canada. Widespread concern about the impact of U.S. firms on that country led, in 1965, to the issuance of "Guidelines for Good Corporate Behavior for Subsidiaries in Canada of Foreign Companies."[1] These guidelines, initially prepared under the direction of Robert Winters, Minister of Trade and Commerce, were updated and reissued in 1975.

Many Canadians feel that the guidelines are ineffective because they are not compulsory.[2] However, several managers of U.S. subsidiaries in Canada agree with one who says: "Winter's guidelines provide the best available baseline for measuring good corporate citizenship in Canada."

International Codes

Both Italy and Canada have been involved in a variety of efforts to develop codes of conduct for multinational enterprises at the international level. As members of the Organization for Economic Cooperation and Development, they took part in the discussions and negotiations which led to the formulation of an O.E.C.D. code of conduct in June, 1976. The code is one part of a broader statement, which also enumerates principles of "national treatment" for foreign-controlled enterprises and identifies official incentives and disincentives for international investment.[3]

In the O.E.C.D. discussions, and in similar exercises carried on in the United Nations, Canada has called attention to its unusual situation as both a major importer and an increasing exporter of capital and, more importantly, as a developed industrial nation which still has many of the characteristics and problems of the developing nations of the world. The Canadian government's position in these discussions has been that, because of this situation, it could not accept an obligation to apply the same standards to domestic and foreign investment.

---

[1] Initially issued by the Ministry of Trade and Commerce (now Department of Industry, Trade, and Commerce) in 1965; reprinted in John Fayerweather, *Foreign Investment in Canada.* White Plains, N.Y.: International Arts and Sciences Press, 1973, Appendix 2.

[2] Fayerweather, pp. 11-12.

[3] New York *Times,* May 27, 1976, p. 1.

Instead, the government insisted that it reserved the right to apply special controls on external investment.

This official position is not universally supported by the Canadian business community. While some business leaders strongly encourage greater government control of foreign investment, others urge that it is greatly in the interest of the growing number of Canadian multinationals to ensure that the principle of national treatment be accepted as widely as possible. One Canadian respondent indicates that the Canadian Business and Industry Advisory Committee (BIAC) was divided over the question of national treatment, some supporting the government's position and others opposing it.

Italian respondents who are familiar with the Canadian posture within the O.E.C.D. express limited sympathy for it. They note that the Canadian dilemma is real—but that Italy, too, could easily show that it is highly industrial on the one hand and economically underdeveloped and dependent on the other. When it comes to issues such as the O.E.C.D. statement of principles however, Italians believe, in the words of one respondent, that "Canada must decide whether it wishes to be considered a modern industrial nation or one of the underdeveloped countries of the Third World." He adds: "Even an industrial country like Canada can become obsessed with the presence of American capital. This can lead to quite irrational behavior."

As one might expect, trade unionists have been particularly interested in and active regarding international codes of conduct. Canadian trade unionists have played a major role in this regard within the International Confederation of Free Trade Unions (ICFTU) and the International Labour Organization (ILO).[4] In the former organization in 1975, Joe Morris, the President of the Canadian Labour Congress, introduced the charter of trade union demands for the legislative control of multinational companies, which was formally adopted by the ICFTU's XI World Congress. Morris described this action as an effort "to devise an international trade union countervailing power to match that of the companies."[5]

The ambivalent posture of the Canadians is also reflected in these activities. Canadian labor leaders themselves note that they have been more active in promoting international codes governing multinational activities in Third World countries than within Canada itself. It is this ambivalence that several Italian respondents underscore.

Italy has been less prominent in these international forums—at least until recently. The Italians took part in the O.E.C.D. negotiations and generally supported the development of the O.E.C.D. code. But they played a relatively quiet role in those procedures. They are concerned that the O.E.C.D. nations not appear to be at odds with each other over the specific content of the guidelines themselves. They believe that it is irrational for the industrial nations to agree to

---

[4] See International Labour Organization, *International Principles and Guidelines on Social Policy for Multinational Enterprises: Their Usefulness and Feasibility*. Geneva: ILO, 1976.

[5] International Confederation of Free Trade Unions (Brussels), *Multinational Charter*, XI World Congress Documents, 1975, p. 8.

hold multinational corporations to standards of conduct that are different from standards applied to national firms. As one Italian diplomat puts it:

"The strange idea emerges that multinationals have only obligations and that nation-states have only rights. The basic byword one hears today, including in places like the European Parliament, is that the multinationals are evil. The multinationals have been made the scapegoat for everything that goes wrong in the Western market system. Generally there is a little question but that the multinationals, both in their parent offices and in the top offices of their affiliates, insist that local laws be obeyed. Attitudes developing in Italy and Europe cannot be ascribed to any violations of laws, or indeed to any specific activities of the affiliates. This does not mean that the multinationals have been without error, or without individual acts of reprehensible behavior. But this is also true of national companies. Such individual acts are not to be ascribed exclusively or particularly to multinationals."

Italian trade unionists on the whole acknowledge that the problems they wish to correct are not peculiar to multinationals and that American multinationals are not to be differentiated from the multinational firms of other industrial countries, including Italy. Nevertheless, these labor leaders are increasingly prominent in efforts to develop a European Communities code of conduct. Communist labor leaders in particular, but those who are Socialists or Christian Democrats as well, believe that such a code is essential. They insist that it would describe corporate obligations not merely toward the countries of the Third World but for any European country as well.[6]

The trade union leaders add that they do not expect that such a code would, in itself, have much impact. But it would become the basis for two other kinds of activity: (1) trade union scrutiny of multinational affiliate practices anywhere in Europe; and (2) pressures on national governments in Europe to enact uniform legislation that would put teeth into any European Communities "code."

Communist party leaders are especially skeptical of international codes. One of them says that while the impulse of certain countries to write an international code is understandable, the code itself will probably add up to zero where the country lacks the political determination to control the multinationals. Where the determination is present, most nations do not require such codes. Where a nation may be weak in imposing its will, even if the will is there, then perhaps a statement at the level of Europe might prove helpful.

In a limiting case, one trade unionist disdainfully writes off international codes as "next to useless." When they come from international bodies, they will have little effect; when they come from corporations, they represent blatant "PR" attempts to convince the public that business managers have social consciences.

Another view is expressed by an editor of one of Italy's leading financial

---

[6] The position of the European Free Trade Union Confederation regarding standards of conduct to which multinationals should be held is delineated in the Appendix to *Syndicats et sociétés multinationales*. Paris: La Documentation Française, 1975, pp. 75-81.

newspapers. He expresses support for an O.E.C.D. code, and for the published "Guidelines" of the International Chamber of Commerce. Asked why, he replies:

"What do these codes do? They cover a number of areas where the lack of state legislation makes possible antisocial behavior by corporations. Sometimes the firms themselves will develop codes and adhere to them as well. They may also give us the kind of information we are after. Codes serve the purpose of showing the public that, even in the absence of state legislation, the corporations themselves are after becoming responsible citizens. A code would remove one basis for public suspicion."

Leading Italian industrialists also anticipate that there may emerge a European Communities code. One of them notes that Italian trade unions are pushing hard in that direction and that they may well have strong input to the eventual content of such a code. He adds that this is another among many reasons why Italy may be a "fascinating laboratory" for foretelling what multinationals will be required to do in the future, and what "social responsibility" may come to mean in Western Europe.

Other industrialists included in our study are less sanguine about a European Communities code, and less convinced that one will emerge. Two of them, whose own companies have developed codes and who have been involved in the evolution of the O.E.C.D. code, stress that industrial nations must avoid accepting any code or statement of expected corporate conduct that does not also delineate the obligation of the host governments in which multinationals operate. Further, they believe that the U.S. government is entirely correct in insisting that multinational firms cannot be held to higher standards of conduct than is expected from indigenous firms.

Two intellectuals, an economist and a sociologist, express skeptical views about international codes. The economist says he does not believe in them a bit, even though he favors harmonized national and European laws and regulations governing multinational enterprise. He believes that the efficacy of these codes will at bottom always be conditioned by the ambivalence of the nation-state toward the multinationals. "Every state," he says, "hopes that the multinational will come in and fears that another country will be chosen."

The sociologist believes these international codes are too abstract. They are not at a level that permits a company to learn what are its obligations in a given national setting. Indeed, the application of such abstract guidelines in some places may turn out to be offensive, unacceptable and counterproductive.

A leading Italian industrialist expresses great doubt that the European Communities or the O.E.C.D. can establish codes of conduct that can in any detailed or specific way establish standard guidelines to be followed by multinationals. He cites as the most obvious example the sphere of industrial relations, where the demands of some European trade unions run up against the widely divergent practices of European countries. Italy, he notes, would be a prominent example of this diversity, given the existence there of a "Workers' Law" that knows no equivalent in Europe. "How can this norm apply everywhere in today's industrial world?'' He goes on to cite the British law on the equality of men and women and wonders whether it would be acceptable to the West Germans. He thinks not. He then adds:

"Even the American trade unions are opposed to setting common standards of industrial relations. For the American unions, the concepts of efficiency and work and of the salary level cannot be separated—a perfectly self-evident idea that seems to be lost on a good many of Europe's trade union leaders. If we don't look out, we will slide into situations where efficiency and profit will be replaced by schemes imposed from above, in which these values are flatly ignored or denied.''

The trade union response, of course, is that these values cannot be considered absolute, or in any case immune to some modification in the interest of maximizing others that are important to the collectivity.

Company Codes

Many of those who react to international codes with caution or skepticism feel somewhat differently about internal company codes of conduct. At the very least, it is urged, such codes serve to remind managers throughout the company of the principal operating norms that presumably govern company behavior. Such codes also serve to alert managers to possible problems that may arise from the company's operations. In some cases, these codes may also raise the consciousness of managers and employees regarding the need to evaluate corporate activities in terms of the wider requirements of social responsibility and corporate citizenship. Where this occurs, there may also occur a greater willingness to take international codes seriously and to explore how conformity with such codes can be made consistent with the responsibilities of managers toward investors.

These same people, however, alert us to a number of potential problems that pertain to individual company codes. In Canada, for example, codes of conduct dictated by the parent company raise typical questions about autonomy. Aspects of these codes remind Canadians of extraterritoriality. Where a given practice is legal, accepted and expected, external prohibitions of it on Canadian citizens and organizations are not necessarily welcomed.

An Italian CEO, whose company has promulgated a worldwide code, agrees that this sort of reaction constitutes a real danger. His solution, and strong recommendation to other firms, is that all overseas affiliates be required to play an active role in the formulation of the code. Otherwise it will represent the "Nth-plus-one" example of "the arrogance of the center."

Canadian managers are sensitive to the need to provide convincing evidence that they are, in fact, highly independent from American headquarters. If company codes erode this posture, or inhibit affiliate adaptability to local conditions, they create more problems than they solve.

The area of political contributions provides a good example of this issue. Corporate political contributions in Canada are legal, well-regulated, and traditional. Recent changes in regulations affecting political contributions seem to ensure complete public disclosure of such contributions. Although some Canadians are unhappy about the way in which political parties have been funded, and in particular about the narrow base of funding, no one suggests that corporations, American or Canadian, have played an illicit role in Canadian politics. Unlike Italy or the United States, corporate political contributions are not a political issue in Canada. On the other hand, American proposals to determine whether Canadian affiliates may make such contributions is exacerbating Canadian feelings about U.S. extraterritoriality.

The autonomy of U.S. subsidiaries, however, is a highly important political issue. Flat prohibitions on political contributions from central headquarters contained in company codes or other directives underline for Canadians the dependent status of subsidiaries there. Canadian managers in several of the affiliates of firms taking part in our study have differing views about corporate contributions to political parties—some are in favor; some oppose. But they all agree that the decision to contribute must be made by Canadian managers, in a Canadian context, and for reasons relevant to Canadian concerns. Good corporate citizenship in Canada is not, they say, bound up with political contributions, one way or the other. It is, however, deeply involved with independence and autonomy.

An interesting example of the potentially wrong balance between costs and benefits of company codes is provided by several U.S. affiliate managers in Italy. For example, one of them wonders whether regional or national headquarters expects them to translate the code accurately into Italian. The reason for this, he says, is that Italians would typically want escape hatches in such wording. He cited Italy's Administrative Code as an example. One can go to it to get a "yes" or a "no" answer for almost any problem or situation.

Another manager says that step number one for those in the United States who write these codes is to assess how a code, once translated abroad, is likely to be viewed and used—or exploited—by various organizations or publics. In Italy, he says, "the very least that people who read our libretto will think is that if we have published it there must be something we are trying to hide!"

A third Italian manager notes that his company code, translated but not yet released in Italy, gives his group reason for pause because it says, in so many words, that his company wants to be an instrument for Italy's economic development. They are fearful, he adds, that the Italian government will interpret that statement as an invitation to exert even greater controls over their industry than already exist. "We may be called on to do 'X' because we said we would be at our country's service." Furthermore he believes that a number of things contained in the code, however well-intentioned and acceptable in the United States, will subject the company to public laughter and ridicule in Italy.

An American official of the American Chamber of Commerce in Italy corroborates that many Italian affiliate managers are at a loss about what to do about the emerging U.S. interest in company codes. They go in to see him and ask: "What am I expected to do with this? What can I possibly do with it? Do they think we're Cleveland?" What they do, he adds, is "make the best of the codes." They will fake it here and there and then report back half truths about what they are doing.

On balance, Italians who favor these codes suggest that they codify what has often been standard expected practice of corporate managers. As such they do have utility. One manager says it is a good idea for any company to put the directives together in a code from time to time. Another says that although his company's unpublished code, which he keeps in the top drawer, prohibits some things that are perfectly acceptable in Italy, he believes occasional annoyances are outweighed by its utility. The code, in his view, helps make it possible for international headquarters to coordinate, regulate and predict managerial behavior in the scores of countries where affiliates are located. A third affiliate manager says he finds it very useful to be able to pull out the company code and say to someone, "No, what you are asking I am forbidden to do."

Italian managers prefer that company codes remain internal documents, and not be published or widely diffused in their country. Canadian managers seem less concerned about allowing company codes to become public insofar as they do not appear to impose rigid centralized controls on Canadian affiliates. It is probable that greater Canadian receptivity also reflects the greater cultural (including business cultural) affinity between Canada and the United States.

Because most of the countries in which American firms operate do not share the full spectrum of Anglo-American norms, it seems essential that managers of overseas affiliates be intimately involved in the development—and in the local adaptation—of company codes. The obvious danger, many times underscored by our respondents, is that these codes will too rigidly reflect the perceptions and values of the parent company, and the American society from which these values derive. On the whole, the potential value of these internal codes seem inextricably tied to how well they succeed in reflecting the values and the expectations of the varied environments in which the multinationals operate. On this important topic, that is the *persistent* and *consistent* message that emerges from the field interviews.

Chapter 11
Extraterritoriality

THE EXTENSION of U.S. law—proposed or on the books—to U.S. corporate affiliates overseas has been a major irritant in Canada and may be on the way to becoming one in Italy. Few issues involving U.S. multinationals in Canada have made life more difficult for affiliate managers. In Italy, affiliate managers and many others begin to wonder exactly how far the United States is prepared to go to prescribe behavior for units incorporated under the laws of the host countries.

Responses to Existing Legislation

In 1968, the Watkins report in Canada focused largely on extraterritoriality. The report noted:

"The most serious cost to Canada of foreign ownership and control results from the tendency of the United States government to regard American-owned subsidiaries as subject to American law and policy with respect to American laws on freedom to export, United States antitrust law and policy, and United States balance of payments policy."[1]

Subsequent studies on foreign investment, such as the Gray Report and the report of the Ontario government's Committee on Economic and Cultural Nationalism, called for stronger measures to prevent the extraterritorial application of U.S. law on or through American-owned subsidiaries in Canada. Gray himself has proposed a legislative regulation that would allow the Canadian government to compel U.S. subsidiaries to ignore orders from its parent.

Gray believes it necessary to terminate past practices whereby Canadian authorities requested, and often got, exemptions from the United States. This has implied a Canadian acceptance of the U.S. position on extraterritoriality, and has implied as well that exemptions are a matter of privilege awarded at the administrative discretion of the United States. What is required, Gray and others believe, is Canadian legislation that flatly denies the right of the United States to have its laws extend north of the border.

These views are widely shared among this study's Canadian respondents. Canadian business leaders, government bureaucrats, trade unionists, and even the managers of U.S.-owned affiliates all agree that U.S. extraterritoriality is the single most serious impediment U.S. firms face in their dealings in Canada. No one says that U.S. multinationals are responsible for this state of affairs. On the other hand, a leading trade unionist states that he "believes it is the responsibility

---

[1] Privy Council Office, *Foreign Ownership and the Structure of Canadian Industry: Report of the Task Force on the Structure of Canadian Industry.* Ottawa, 1968, p. 360.

of U.S. firms to put pressure on the American government to end this sort of behavior.''

The shoe is occasionally on the other foot. Two or three Canadians call attention to certain extraterritorial implications of Canada's current foreign investment review process. If, for example, one U.S. firm wants to sell its wholly owned Canadian affiliate to another American firm, it must still be reviewed by the Canadian government. A leading nationalist comments that an ''unexpected silver lining'' of the review legislation was to provide this ''second crack at U.S. firms and to enlarge Canadian benefits.''

Trading with the Enemy Act

In past years, the most irritating aspect of this problem centered on the U.S. Trading with the Enemy Act. Great furor and confusion was raised some years ago over whether a U.S. subsidiary in Canada could sell trucks and other products to the People's Republic of China or, more recently, to Cuba. The emotional storms which resulted highlight how deeply such legislation can wound the pride of another people. One Canadian observes that he ''like many other Canadians, would not have supported Canadian trade with Cuba. But because of the pressure of the United States, I was forced to support the right of Canadians to trade wherever they pleased.''

The specific issue of selling to the enemies of the United States is now more symbolic than it was a few years ago. But the residue of the issue has been—and is—enormous. Robert Perry, in his book on the ''American presence'' in a Canadian city, quotes a Canadian trade unionist:

''Those accursed trucks that Canada couldn't sell to China: they've worked their way into conventional lore, like Ookpik and Ogopogo. They've become the focus of all the familiar, popular, predictable rhetoric about the extraterritorial extension of American law into Canada.''[2]

Antitrust

Canadian affiliate managers we interviewed are more concerned now about U.S. antitrust legislation. Among other things, they stress that American laws could collide head-on with Canadian efforts to rationalize industry. The Canadians note that one reason for the continued anemic position of industry in Canada is the failure to bring about economies of scale. Achieving this in a number of highly fragmented industrial sectors would, they say, require exactly the kinds of combines that might catch the attention and win the ire of the Antitrust Division of the U.S. Justice Department. They believe that this obstacle must be overcome. Managers of one Canadian subsidiary in this study observe that a noteworthy benefit of their fully Canadianized management and board of directors is that, as Canadian citizens, they cannot be held subject to U.S. law on such matters.

[2] Robert L. Perry, *Galt, U.S.A.* Toronto: Maclean-Hunter Ltd., 1971, p. 42.

Italians also mention antitrust. Several leading industrialists, managers of U.S. affiliates, economists and journalists say that these laws must not be extended to Italy. Among their effects, they say, is the reluctance (however misplaced) of certain American affiliates to join Italian industrial associations. Often as not, affiliate managers explain their failure to sign up by referring to the Justice Department. Italians reply that this isolation is part and parcel of failure to integrate into the local society; prime evidence of bad, not good corporate citizenship. In some cases, the isolation of foreign companies from their own association may lead to exactly the kinds of activities and later complications that befell members of Italy's Unione Petrolifera (Petroleum Union).

Italian respondents sometimes refer to Trading with the Enemy legislation as a carry-over from McCarthyism and the Cold War. They add that such extension of U.S. laws provides a basis for fearing the U.S. firm, not as such but as an instrument of American international ambitions.

A severe Italian critic captures the spirit of much of what was said:

"A series of laws and regulations from Washington imposes on multinationals of American parentage behavior that can only perturb and irritate European governments. All of these foreign affiliates are held above all to certain commercial laws (and, one must add, not all of them are bad) that are different from the laws of European states. Thus affiliates of American firms in Europe must conform, for example, to American regulations on the balance of payments. Which means in practice that the Treasury Department determines the amount of profit they are compelled to transfer."[3]

Although Italians have been less exercised than Canadians about extraterritoriality, we are told that this situation will change. One strategy will be to make it illegal for Italian citizens, and therefore managers of U.S. multinational affiliates, to furnish the U.S. government with certain kinds of information regarding corporate activities. In a country where information disclosure about corporate activity is already quite rare and problematic, says one financial editor, such legislation would be entirely lamentable.

Response to Current Proposals

Italy's most recent interest in extraterritoriality is spurred by hearings of the Securities and Exchange Commission and of the U.S. Senate subcommittee on multinational corporations. Italians are baffled by what they feel to be an excessive American penchant for public confessions and public atonement. Most Italians interviewed point out that there would be immensely less furor in Italy about U.S. multinationals there were it not for the U.S. Senate and S.E.C. investigations, the massive reporting in the U.S. press, and the transmission to Italy of politically volatile documents from the Senate committee.

[3] Angelo Genari, "La presenza delle imprese multinazionali in Italia nei diversi settori produttivi," *Quaderni di azione sociale,* No. 4/6, 1973, pp. 29-30.

An Italian CEO of a major U.S. firm expresses himself unequivocally about exposés that come to Italy from the United States:

"Why doesn't Senator Church consent to having some of his accusations probed more deeply? Why doesn't he come here to Italy to talk with the people who have to take the brunt of what he says in the United States? Why is he satisfied to tell only part of the story? Why doesn't he show the courage to come and pursue right to the bottom some of the ideas he has about the multinationals?"

Even several of Italy's Communist Party leaders wonder what could be the interest of American officials in exposing American companies abroad to the kinds of attacks that come on the heels of revelations elicited by the S.E.C. and the Senate subcommittee. One of them says that he does not approve, certainly, of assassination plots, heavy-handed political use of money, and so on. He adds that it is nevertheless disconcerting to observe the statesmen and major newspapers of a great nation behaving in a self-destructive way.

Those Italians who express admiration that the U.S. can openly pursue these exposures nevertheless express deep reservations about American legislative proposals designed to restrict further the activities of U.S. corporate affiliates abroad. They point out that contributions to political parties in Italy, for example, is standard practice for all large-scale corporations and that it is disingenuous for anyone in a position of responsibility, in Italy or elsewhere, to claim unawareness of this. Similarly, in Canada several respondents note in the matter of U.S. corporate contributions to political parties, that it is not only legal but also expected that such support will be provided. Official U.S. prohibition of these activities will cause far more difficulty for U.S. firms than to continue present policies.

In sum, Italians react to the legislative proposals that follow on the heels of recent investigations as one more example of the arrogant insensitivity of the United States toward other countries. Trade unionists and industrialists, Communists and Christian Democrats, journalists and academics, bureaucrats and ministers of government express astonishment at the bland way in which Americans take it as a foregone conclusion that they can legislate behavior of organizations and foreign nationals located outside the jurisdiction of the United States.

One of our respondents summed it up this way:

"The fact is that Senator Church really believes he can transfer to Italy American norms regarding corporation and political parties. I do not see how American affiliates in Italy can respect these norms, and I assume that, one way or another, they will be rejected. If I'm not mistaken Senator Church is not the Senator from Florence or Palermo."

A former prime minister and person of extensive governmental experience expresses an even stronger view, holding it to be "reckless and mischievous" for members of the U.S. legislature to transmit to Italy, knowing that they will be exploited politically, accusations and innuendoes that fall short of the whole story, and cannot be contested in regular judicial proceedings. ''Accusations and allegations of this kind can only have mischievous consequences from the standpoint of the United States and the West, and those who are interested in preserving Italian democracy.'' [4]

[4] We might add that this respondent is not among those Italians suspected of receiving payments from American corporations. If we interviewed ''Antelope Cobbler'' in this study, this fact is unknown to us at this time.

Part Four:
Conclusions and Prospects

Chapter 12
Summary of Findings

THE FINDINGS of this study fall into two main categories:

• Those dealing with the issue of the broader impact of multinational firms on host-country economies.
• Those associated with the particular operations of the multinational firm within a given host country.

Canadian and Italian elites are unequivocal in acknowledging the contributions that U.S. firms have made to the economic and industrial development of their respective countries. Without the interventions of direct American investment, Canadian and Italian elites stress that their countries would not be among the world's advanced industrial nations. Moreover, in both countries the overwhelming majority of those interviewed believe that the continued presence of U.S. firms there is highly desirable. (See Chapter 3.)

Nevertheless, many of our respondents are concerned that high levels of dependence on foreign capital may limit indigenous control over the precise direction that national development may take. It is noteworthy that this fear is not appreciably greater in Canada, where American capital has massive impact on the economy, than in Italy, where the relative weight of foreign direct investment is much lighter. Italians point out that the *particular industrial sector* where foreign capital is found is a critical consideration. Because they find a very strong American presence in exactly those sectors considered vital to further industrial development, many of the Italian elites express a consternation similar to the Canadians'.

In both countries, then, elites express deep concern about patterns of ownership, and about the possibility that future economic development at home may be overly dependent on investment decisions taken outside their respective countries. They stress that existing distributions of foreign investment and prevailing modes of equity ownership may create permanent second-class status for their countries. They assure us that there will be increasing public and governmental attention to this problem.

There are three major expected consequences predicted by this study's respondents that require underscoring here. First, there are likely to be increased pressures for new equity arrangements. The time is past when either of these countries will passively accept equity arrangements dictated by foreign firms or governments. The wholly owned subsidiary arrangement will come under increased scrutiny and criticism; there will be greater demands for joint ventures, including ventures with industrial and financial institutions in the public sector of host countries. Italy's Institution for Industrial Reconstructions (IRI), one of the largest holding companies in the world, will aggressively seek such joint ventures. In

Canada there is strong interest in requiring at least minority share ownership by Canadian citizens or institutions. (See Chapter 4.)

A second expected change involves research and development. (See Chapter 5.) The more knowledgeable Canadian and Italian elites recognize that this is not a simple problem, easily resolved by applying pat formulas about *how much* R and D should be conducted abroad. Questions of interest to these elites include such items as:

(1) Who determines what form R and D will take in the parent company and abroad? In particular, how much overseas autonomy and/or input does there exist regarding investments in R and D?

(2) How can one better assess the relative cost and benefits of R and D to parent and host countries in which the multinationals operate?

(3) How can host-country governments play a more direct and determining role in establishing how much R and D is done overseas in critical sectors like data processing and electronics?

(4) How can R and D be structured abroad so that it helps to stimulate the development of scientific and technological infrastructure in host countries?

(5) What can be done to ensure that R and D conducted abroad will permit the development of internationally competitive product lines, thus helping the balance of payments problems of host countries?

It is noteworthy that Italians do not expect or insist that each American firm operating there develop a local R and D facility. They acknowledge the imperatives of scale and of critical mass in this sector. They add, however, that more installation of *basic* research facilities somewhere within countries making up the European Communities is highly desirable and will probably be required in the future.

A third consequence will involve efforts of Canadians and Italians to control in greater detail the conditions under which direct investment will be permitted and, once allowed, how long the investor will be required to remain in the host country. Italians express great interest in Canadian and Japanese legislation in this area. Some Canadians, on the other hand, believe that the government can and should be more demanding than it has thus far been in the administration of the laws governing foreign investment.

Italians are particularly concerned with the so-called "politics of disinvestment." Many of them, including those who might be expected to oppose capitalism, lament decisions of American and other multinationals to abandon Italy. At the very least, they want regulations that will minimize the harmful effects of corporate decisions to get out and go elsewhere. A fair number of Italian elites recognize that a necessary condition for achieving this goal is the establishment of a more coherent public policy regarding foreign investors, and a more realistic and less unattractive system of industrial relations. (See Chapter 6.)

There are substantial and vital differences between Canadians and Italians about control issues. Canadians see economic control as one dimension of the wider issue of Canada's autonomy and independence as a nation, especially vis-à-vis the

United States. Italians, on the other hand, are more likely to see the European system as the major counterbalance to the threat of external control. Differences, however, matter less than similarities. In both countries, elites feel that the price of the contribution of U.S. multinational firms to national economic development cannot be the effective loss of control over that process of development. Past needs for U.S. capital and know-how were so great and other factors, such as the international political situation, so critical that questions of control could be overlooked, at least in the short run. But this era no longer exists, and the sheer expansion of the American presence abroad has made the question of control unavoidable. Canadians feel that Canada must be able to weigh the costs of economic benefits more carefully, and to insist that the loss of control over national destinies not be a cost of the continued U.S. economic presence. Italians agree, although some prefer to look to Europe rather than Italy alone to maintain economic and national autonomy.

A number of more specific findings, relating to operational issues for the MNC in the host country, stand out. These range from expectations about indigenous managers, to the role of the MNC in the host community, to problems of political sensitivity. Both Canadians and Italians expect that, if senior positions in U.S. subsidiaries are not yet held by indigenous managers, they soon will be. The use of local managers at the very highest levels is seen generally—though not universally—as a basic element of good corporate citizenship abroad. However desirable and praiseworthy this may be, and however vital to the development of local management cadres, this pattern also carries some serious problems. (See Chapter 7.)

Our findings show that the use of indigenous managers creates various job and career expectations which parent headquarters cannot always fulfill, particularly when local managers are increasingly reluctant to leave their own countries to advance their careers in the firm. The evidence strongly suggests that the concept of dual identity and allegiance on the part of corporate managers—i.e., national and corporate "citizenship"—is essentially a myth. Basic identities, loyalties, perceptions, values and evaluations remain closely tied to the nationality of the individual corporate manager. Contrary to what many may believe, the multinational corporation has had relatively little impact on this basic reality.

The use of indigenous managers should not be confused with the decentralization or devolution of decisional authority. Indeed, there is some slight evidence that the use of indigenous managers means that the parent company will extend less decisional autonomy to the affiliate than is the case where overseas managers are Americans. In any case, the Canadian example clearly reveals that the nearly total utilization of host-country nationals in subsidiaries there does not solve the problem of local control. By and large, parent companies still severely circumscribe the autonomy of local managers, whether Canadian or not.

Italians and Canadians (the latter are particularly outspoken on this point) are widely opposed to subsidiaries being treated as merely "branch plants," and they urge that local affiliates be enabled to perform the fullest possible range of activities. Affiliate demands for such autonomy are, of course, not new. But these tensions between parent and affiliates are likely to be heightened by changing attitudes in host countries such as those described earlier in this chapter. Moreover, the evidence from our research suggests that affiliate managers themselves will become increasingly articulate and insistent in demanding greater autonomy. Such demands will be particularly thoughtworthy in the light of some of the potential organizational developments discussed in Chapter 13.

Generally U.S. firms in Italy and Canada have few labor and industrial relations problems that arise because they are multinationals. Not only do respondents give the multinationals high marks in this area; they often add that the American firms set exemplary patterns that local firms (particularly in Italy) would do well to emulate. (See Chapter 8.)

On the other hand, some Italian labor leaders feel that U.S. firms are particularly loath to come to terms with the new philosophy of industrial relations that emerged in Italy in 1969, and which may be emerging elsewhere in Western Europe as well. In both Italy and Canada, moreover, the alleged overcentralization of the multinationals is said to make their affiliates abroad less sensitive to local needs and interests than they might be. Some elites suggest that lack of sensitivity is fundamentally bad for business, particularly when it means that products are inadequately adapted to local marketing conditions. More importantly, overcentralization is said to prevent local affiliates from playing a more active and positive role in the host country's efforts to achieve its goals.

One of the most widespread Canadian and Italian criticisms is that U.S. affiliates do not take a more active role in the host community and that they are not sufficiently involved in the life of the nation in which they live. (See Chapter 9.) In their dealings with host governments, U.S. firms are seen to conform to national styles and patterns. Recent revelations in the United States of bribery and other corporate misbehavior deeply concern our respondents, but few characterize U.S. MNC's in general as the worst offenders.

Criticism is greater, though, of the typical "low profile" approach of many U.S. firms abroad. Even friendly critics state this is like "trying to hide an elephant in a bathroom," and that this is bound to increase suspicion of these firms. U.S. MNC's suffer from a lack of credibility and a "low profile" worsens the situation. On the other hand, those multinationals that have succeeded in avoiding open identification as U.S. firms often have affiliate managers who prefer it this way. This especially is the case at a time when U.S. firms are under public fire both abroad and in the United States itself.

Both countries have taken part in efforts at the international, national and corporate levels to develop codes of conduct for MNC's. Uncertainty was expressed about the impact of such codes. Canadians have been more active in this process, but have deeply ambivalent attitudes about the applicability of international codes to their own country. Generally, most respondents hope that the creation of international codes, by both international organizations and multinationals, will serve to heighten awareness of the problems existing between the MNC's and their hosts. Yet many of the respondents remain highly skeptical about the effectiveness of such codes. (See Chapter 10.)

It was noted with great interest that the most severe criticism regarding U.S. MNC's in Italy and Canada is not directed at the firms but, rather, at the respondents' governments for failing to develop more effective policies for dealing with foreign multinationals within the context of overall national economic and industrial policies. The interviews show that there is also a very deep hostility, especially in Canada but in Italy as well, to the extraterritorial application of U.S. law either on or through the foreign subsidiaries of U.S. firms. (See Chapter 11.) Whatever benefits may accrue to the United States from extraterritoriality here, the costs have been extremely high. Furthermore, some of the overseas hostility directed at U.S. multinationals reflects antagonism to the United States as a world power and not simply to the multinationals as such.

In general it was found that U.S. firms fail to use politically relevant information effectively in their decision making. In the first case, knowledge about sources of this information is limited. In particular, little use is made of U.S. governmental agencies abroad. U.S. firms do not normally maintain regular contacts with or solicit politically relevant information from U.S. diplomatic and consular officials. At the same time, it does not appear that U.S. government agencies and embassies encourage firms to make or maintain such contacts. One reason for this seems to be that the Federal Government is less equipped than it might be to provide the kinds of services needed. Another is that locally recruited affiliate managers do not naturally turn to the U.S. government for assistance.

Secondly, it appears that little political analysis or forecasting goes into longer term corporate planning. It was felt this may be the most urgent requirement facing U.S. MNC's in their operations abroad. On the whole, respondents suggest that, in the medium and longer run, multinationals must make efforts to improve their capacities to assess changing political and social patterns in host countries, to forecast alternative futures and options for the firm, and to integrate these assessments and forecasts into corporate planning.

In both Canada and Italy, nations with long traditions of liberal policies toward foreign capital, the relationships between the public and private sectors of their economies are undergoing substantial changes as they strive to develop economic and industrial policies appropriate to perceived political and social requirements of the coming decade. Neither Canadians with nationalistic feelings nor Italian Communists represent a political fringe; to an increasing extent their ideas and policies have moved into the mainstream of politics in the two countries.

It is felt that U.S. firms are insufficiently aware of the need to develop more sensitive political and social assessment capacities, or have given insufficient thought to the creation of mechanisms for information gathering and assessment. In the past, such capacities were rarely required. But in environments like those in Canada and Italy today, in which political and economic structures as well as policies are undergoing rapid and extensive change (which have particular impact on the operations of U.S. firms there), the interviews show that the need for such assessment capacities has increased enormously. Without this, the cost of operations will be excessively high.

Chapter 13
Multinationals and the Future

IN THIS concluding chapter we will treat several topics raised, but not elaborated on, in earlier sections. First, the likely directions of Canadian and Italian policies toward American foreign investment. Second, the nature and future prospect of what Italians and others are calling the "Eurostrategy" toward American multinationals. Third, the interesting organizational alternatives—or imperatives—that the top managers of American multinationals should be considering.

Future Policies toward U.S. Investment

Elites in Canada and Italy not only expect that policies toward the multinationals will change; many of them are actually demanding this, and spelling out what should be the content of new public policies. Canadians, as we have seen, are far ahead of Italians in the use of public instrumentalities to oversee and to regulate the uses to which foreign capital is put internally. Many of those in Italy who lament the absence of a coherent national policy hold up Canada as a model. However, some Italians (particularly those on the Left) believe that the Canadians have not gone far enough. They agree with those Canadians who say that, so far at least, the Foreign Investment Review Agency has been a relatively innocuous form of government control with a markedly limited mandate. Canadians themselves often express unhappiness that the FIRA screening process has been so liberal, and they urge that the agency be more vigorously used to keep out undesirable foreign investment.

When Canadian and Italian elites who are unhappy with existing policies are asked what kinds of specific new policies they would recommend or prefer, a number of items surface—most of them indicated in earlier chapters. In both countries there is demand for full-cycle operations in the manufacturing sector. Both Canadians and Italians add that this must include much more decentralization of research and development to their countries than has so far been the case. There will be pressures for equity sharing in both countries, although stronger in Canada than in Italy because of the relative weakness of the private investment sector in the latter country. In Italy, on the other hand, those elites who hold top positions in the public industrial and financial sectors are likely to generate great pressure for joint ventures involving publicly controlled enterprise. American government officials in Italy may well be asked to facilitate such arrangements.

Canadians and Italians believe that the government must be much more eagle-eyed in determining whether a proposed new investment adds significantly to what may already exist in each country by way of enterprise; whether there are sufficient amounts of *outside* capital involved in investment proposals; whether the value-added dimension of foreign direct investment is reasonably clear-cut. Italians will no doubt be much more vigilant to prevent *investimenti di rapina*. In view of the drama and trauma associated with the recent spate of disinvestment efforts and decisions, many Italians feel that firms that decide they want entry to Italy will have to agree to stay a minimum number of years.

A number of Italian elites complain that American multinational affiliates often do not bring to the country the most advanced technology available in the United States. We heard none of this from Canadian elites, perhaps because Canadians are geographically closer to the United States and able to assess whether there is such a discrepancy. In any case, it is interesting that a number of our respondents in Italy single out the food and food-processing sector as an alleged example of this problem; the agricultural machinery sector was identified as another.

Taken as a group of more or less shared criticisms of the past and demands for the future, the attitudes of many Italian elites add up to saying that there should be more conscious national economic planning and that a carefully worked out industrial development policy should be given a prominent place in any national plan. Many Canadians agree, but would be more likely to shy away from the word "plan," preferring "strategy."

Once the national—and perhaps regional or provincial—governments move in that rationalizing direction, then basic questions about the presence of direct foreign investment can be posed and resolved. At that point, as a leading Italian economist notes, the government can decide whether it wants multinationals around at all; what kinds of multinationals it wishes to encourage or discourage; exactly what it expects from such foreign investors; and also what the country itself will have to do in order to encourage foreign investors to agree to be present.

Both in Italy and in Canada there are forces at work designed to redefine the relationship between the private and the public sectors. The Canadian issue goes to the heart of the traditional liberal posture of the government in the economic sphere. That posture has involved public-sector attention to the infrastructural needs for economic development and not much more. Traditionally the relationship between government and business has been minimal; the government, as one Canadian respondent puts it, has been considered the holder of the ring and the nightwatchman. In recent years and months, however, our Canadian respondents indicate a more conscious tendency toward greater interventionist policies. One Canadian manager says these changing attitudes appear to show that in the extractive sector "Canadians seem to prefer Canadian public ownership to U.S. private ownership." Other affiliate managers there underscore the growing interest of Canadian governmental authorities in helping firms work out the development of international product specialization.

A highly placed Canadian public servant says that the "ground rules are changing around the world," that there is increasing pressure for direct government involvement in a wide range of industrial activities. The current pressures on the multinationals must be understood to be only a dimension of the much wider changes that may be occurring in the relationship between the public and private sectors.

Although Italy's massive public-sector ownership of industrial capacity makes that country appear less liberal in comparison with Canada, in fact this has not been the case. Until very recent times, the government may have owned but it certainly did not consciously manage large-scale industries in conjunction with an explicit developmental policy. Fundamentally, Italian governments have followed a liberal, hands-off policy toward all industrial enterprise, whether in the public or the private sector. This policy has been the basis for perhaps the most insistent attack from those on the Left (and even certain Christian Democrats) who demand a much more interventionist governmental role. Elites (including Socialists) who criticize the Socialist Party's failures under the so-called "Opening to the Left" that began in 1962 center this attack on the Socialists' lack of attention to the problem of changing the role of government in directing the economy. They now expect that things will be fundamentally different on this score if and when the Communists come to share power in Italy.

Before we examine the Italian Communist Party's position in all of this, we should note that factors persist in both Canada and Italy that would *not* encourage more public-sector intervention than has existed in the past and, therefore, not as much additional interference with direct foreign investment as many of the elites would like. In Canada the traditional liberal position is anything but moribund. FIRA for example is criticized for providing too much room for administrative discretion as well as for creating the possibility for political maneuvering. At least one recent ruling dealing with the Westinghouse Electric Company gives some credence to this view.[1] The investment review process is scored as too time-consuming and too costly for the firms involved.

The backlash also involves stepped-up criticisms of too much "dirigisme," too much "socialism." One Canadian executive, a traditional conservative nationalist, fears that the increasingly "socialistic" policies of the Canadian government will lead U.S. firms to tighten controls on their Canadian subsidiaries and to limit their autonomy.

Italy's liberal voices are much more muted than those in Canada. Nevertheless, there are many in Italy—including leading figures of the Left—who want any further attempts on the part of the public sector to interfere with or to direct the private sector to proceed with great caution. Those Italians who are deeply concerned about disinvestment are loath to have the government step in with stiff regulations that may cause a snowballing of that phenomenon. An Italian puts it this way:

" ...it is when they leave (a possibility that in the classical controversies of a few years ago wasn't even considered) that, in terms of employment, production gaps, and the weighting down of industrial structures, they [MNC's] create the greatest damage."[2]

One of the economists we interviewed in this study has written quite pointedly about the question of more controls. He notes that, whereas Italy has argued the

---

[1] On this ruling, see *Business Week*, April 19, 1976, pp. 42-3.
[2] Girolamo Fiori, "Vivere con l'elefante," *Mondo economico*, January 31, 1976, p. 6.

most polemically about the multinationals, it has also introduced fewest controls by comparison with other European countries. If Italy is now considering taking steps to ammortize the cost of having multinationals there, these steps refer to the public sector's concerns about *all* large-scale industry, not merely the multinationals.[3] He adds that if a country imposes additional controls and an existing multinational with affiliates there decides to stay, it can be predicted that the multinational will play by the new rules. One must add, however, that top management will take the existence of controls into account in its decision making and will treat them exactly as it would other factors of incentive and disincentive relating to company operations (existing or prospective) in a given country.

In effect, Canadians and Italians want greater controls effected over direct foreign investors, but not to the extent that controls would seriously deplete needed capital outlays from outside. The last thing Italian elites want is to force the multinationals out. As a trade unionist who is among the severest critics of private enterprise puts it: "Now, the idea that the multinationals can be combatted by getting rid of them is very much like the story of the savage before fire. You shouldn't put out the fire; you should learn to harness it."

For Canada, the spectrum of possible future policy options is more limited than in Italy. There is some feeling in certain parts of the Canadian government that the foreign investment review process should represent the beginning of a more discretionary and selective approach to dealings with the private sector, and especially with foreign investors and firms. It is urgent, say some respondents, that the Canadian government become more skilled in dealing with foreign firms and that the review process provide additional benefits in training the government to negotiate with them.

Indeed, one respondent states, the purpose of FIRA is *essentially* educational. It is not designed to keep out foreign investment, he says, but to improve the benefits of foreign investment for Canada, by educating Canadian government officials and foreign businessmen to Canadian needs and demands. For foreign firms, he continues, "this may be the beginning of social responsibility."

It is unlikely that the policy of free trade recently called for by the Economic Council of Canada will find much in-depth support at this time. It is probably true, as several Canadians suggest, that this position has more support in principle than it appears to have. But few Canadians are really prepared to take the risks involved in actually putting such a policy into effect.

In general, there will probably be a continued mix of pragmatic policies in Canada that affect the U.S. MNC. The foreign investment review process will be broadened, although it will probably also be made more open and more efficient; there will be continued gradual lessening of tariffs; more government-sponsored rationalization in various industrial sectors; continued efforts to work out closer economic relations with the Common Market and Japan; and attempts, more or less likely to succeed, to create some national policy on resources.

---

[3] Franco Momigliano, "Sempre imprese, dopotutto," *Mondo economico,* January 31, 1976, pp. 12-15.

Without doubt, pressure will increase on U.S. MNC's to demonstrate that they are providing greater benefits to Canada. Canadians are of one mind on this basic requirement.

Finally, at least for the foreseeable future, "continentalist" options will remain ruled out, even if they have high economic rationality. To judge by our interviews, north-south economic linkages, even on a sector-by-sector basis, are not very likely. In the longer run, however, Canadian fears of isolation may prevail over nationalism. Canada cannot exist as an industrial nation outside of the European Common Market and cut off from the United States. Its domestic market of some 22 millions simply will not support the weight. It is quite possible that, in the long run, some sort of "continental logic" will become more respectable. Much will depend, in the meanwhile, on the way in which the U.S. government and American MNC's deal with Canada and on the tact, skill and—once again—sensitivity they show in these dealings.

Italian Communists and the Multinationals

This brings us to a consideration of how the Italian Communists would treat the multinationals—if and when they have official authority and power to make policy in this area. Eleven Communist leaders were interviewed in Italy, some of them more than once. This group includes several members of the party's Central Committee, a prominent member of its executive, several specialists concerned with economics and foreign relations, several trade unionists and members of Parliament, and several regional leaders. As field work in Italy was concluded, we were also given an advance copy of a statement that will represent the Communist Party's official position regarding the role of foreign capital under the economic and industrial development policy the party espouses.

Without exception, Communist leaders say that their proposed policies, and their conception of economic planning, do not exclude a role for foreign direct investment. Indeed, they note that it would not be possible for Italy to push ahead for long with further industrial development were the sources of such investment to dry up, or even markedly to diminish.

Obviously, the Communists would impose greater controls, more stringent restrictions. These would *not* be tied to a system of highly centralized economic planning, which the Italian Communists openly reject. In fact, they are committed to high degrees of regional autonomy in planning and development. They talk about public and private agencies in the regions becoming "collective consumers" that would produce stable and predictable demands for the products of industry, including multinational industry. Within a set of developmental priorities set by the nation, there would be considerable flexibility. Communist leaders express the hope that the multinational structures of the future will be able to adapt in a mutually attractive and profitable way.

The Communists clearly want more order and predictability. Industrial firms, one leader says, "cannot be permitted to continue to function in a situation of anarchy." He goes on:

"We cannot permit firms to do exactly as they like; to make foreign exchange deals as they may desire; or basically to go their own way without any interference from state authority. The state must have a policy. Economic development requires that investments and other basic processes come under greater supervision and control than has been the case so far."

Communists say they would not limit demands for less anarchy to the corporate sphere. They recognize that there is much that requires rationalizing on the labor and trade union side, and they tell us privately (but have not yet said this in so many words publicly) that they are prepared to be severe in this sector, too. A leader says in this regard:

"We believe that today the working class in Italy is prepared to accept sacrifices. It will take a long time to put Italy back in shape. Unlike the French Communist Party, we think we can and must ask the workers (but not *only* the workers) to accept sacrifices in the interest of bringing about the rebirth of the country. Otherwise you may be sure that the game is lost."

Communists say they want reforms that proceed within a democratic framework, that the kind of economic recovery they are after requires that it proceed within a democratic and not a Soviet-type framework. Furthermore, they are explicit that recovery can, will and must proceed within the context of a "dual economy" in which the market will play a central role, and in which the multinational enterprise will be centrally present as well. They add that, from the standpoint of multinational decision making, the order and predictability they would try to bring about in the country would be entirely attractive.

In effect, every Communist interviewed comes around to saying that the party accepts both democratic pluralism and the market. During the course of one interview, it was suggested to the distinguished Communist leader involved that his remarks about these things, and about the role of the private sector in development, sounded as though they might easily have been made by Adam Smith. He replied: "Adam Smith is OK with me, but don't confuse us with the Social Democrats."

What kinds of specific limits would the Communists set? They are very much like those articulated by others and noted above. They make a special point of excluding foreign investments that are largely marketing operations in Italy. They will oppose takeovers limited to financial transactions designed to turn a profit without bringing a discernible added value to the country. They will clearly want much more vigilance over capital flows, and will drive harder bargains on the repatriation of profits.

What about nationalization? The respondents, again without exception, say that the party is generally opposed to further nationalization of enterprise and that, if anything, it believes there has been too much of it in Italy. Some observers outside the party in fact tell us that the Communists might actually favor returning certain industries to the private sector. Socialist respondents are critical on both scores.

They often charge that the Italian Communist Party (PCI) is prepared, for entirely opportunistic reasons, to sacrifice some of the sacred tenets of Marxism. Communists reply that they have for years demonstrated that they do not consider the writings of Marx and Lenin to be holy tenets, nor will they permit them to become operational straitjackets.

Many persons, in and out of Italy, have found these pronouncements surprising. Some of the respondents in this study brush them aside as strictly tactical, holding that the Communists are simply reaching for power and will behave quite differently once they get it. One minister of government asks us to consider that "Berlinguer is the lamb today but will be the bear tomorrow."

Eugenio Peggio, a leading economic policy maker for the PCI, provides one response to these reactions, articulated in 1975 at a meeting of the National Convention for Labor Civilization. He said:

"The originality of the posture taken by the PCI, which does not think that further nationalization of private firms is necessary . . . , has triggered wonderment, and sometimes even ironical reactions. But this posture is not a sign of a tactical, contingent position. . . . It goes back to the PCI position at the [nation's] Constituent Assembly."

Peggio is also the author of the PCI's most recent statement of industrial and economic developmental policy, scheduled to be published later in 1976.[4] That statement contains such major points as these:

(1) That Italy must reach for greater economic autonomy, less dependence on countries like the United States, but without falling into the entrapment of economic nationalism and, even worse, autarchy.

(2) That multinational firms are not to be outlawed in Italy's future planning for industrial reconversion and development. But the state must ensure that these firms contribute substantially to developmental plans and that they be impeded from engaging in corrupt practices.

(3) That Canada, France and Japan offer important examples of the kinds of requirements that Italy may wish in the future to impose on multinationals.

(4) That no evaluation of the value or contribution of any firm, including the multinational firm, can be made unless and until there is a national policy describing a precise strategy of national development.

Most of the other Italian elites interviewed, as well as Italian managers of American firms in Italy, are prepared to take the oft-repeated Communist reassurances at face value. They note that the Communists dread that their coming to power in Italy might reproduce the "Chilean scenario"; they point out that the Communists are well aware that neither the Soviet Union nor the countries of

---

[4] Eugenio Peggio, "Relazione introduttiva," in CESPE, *Crisi economica e condizionamenti internazionali dell' Italia* (forthcoming).

Eastern Europe are able to produce the external capital—to say nothing of the industrial know-how—that further economic development in Italy requires. A leading Communist puts it in a nutshell: ''We know what the international rules of finance and investment are, and you Americans will have to recognize that we are willing and able to play by them.'' Another adds, ''Basically, Italy is going to be a safer and more predictable place for the multinationals. They will simply have to understand our rules and abide by them.''

A leading Socialist adds:

''The day the Communist Party comes to power in this country, it will represent the first serious and modern and able government Italy has had. What I would expect is that they will approach the kinds of problems we have been discussing today from the standpoint of objective, although very vigorous, analysis. There is really very little to fear from them.''

Italian industrialists who represent the largest Italian multinational firms, leaders of Italy's industrial associations at Milan and Rome, high-level bureaucrats who deal with industrial problems on a day-to-day basis, even the most important leaders of the Liberal Party take essentially the same view. How far can we rely on these views?

First, a number of respondents say that the Communist Party's ability to discipline organized labor, or to run too far ahead of its own members and militants should not be overestimated. These latter can be expected to produce a loud clamor for populist policies that would imply, for example, more direct worker control of the firm and more ''disciplining'' of the multinationals. One individual points out, for example, that the Communist leaders cannot expect that the masses will sit around and blandly accept the philosophy summarized above after the party has for decades attacked private enterprise and the United States as the source of all domestic and international evil. Another Italian leader—a former minister and prominent Socialist—says that such populist demands are inevitable but that most of the anti-U.S. and antimultinational outpouring will turn out to be verbiage, rhetoric. The important thing will be for the United States and its industrial managers to avoid ''losing their cool.''

Second, *what kind of multinational we are discussing* will evidently make some difference. Where extractive industries like petroleum are concerned, the rhetoric is predictably going to reach a much higher pitch. A few Italian respondents believe that Italy might slide into nationalizing that sector, however irrational and unnecessary that step might be, however much the Communists themselves might wish to avoid it.

Communists themselves tend to make an exception of firms involved in the energy field, broadly conceived. One of them, a specialist on energy problems, says that they will work to slow down the Italian government's tendency to keep American industries dominant in this sphere. They indicate that we can expect recent efforts to broaden the international competition in the area of nuclear power to be stepped up.

In this sense, we might add, there is an interesting parallel to draw between Italy and Canada. There is very little talk among Canadians about "buy-back" arrangements, and even less about nationalization. Canadians, like Italians who oppose buy-back, assume there are better uses to which the capital involved might be put.

Third, it is clear that although Italian Communists do not despair of the nation's ability to control the multinationals, they add that controls would be all the more effective if they could be exercised at the international level—on the basis of much tighter cooperation among nations that make up the European Communities.

The Eurostrategy of Italian Communism

One of the most fascinating findings from our field work involves the extent of the Communist leadership's commitment to the institutions of the Common Market, and to the idea that all effort must be made to strengthen them. One of those interviewed indicates that he is involved in polemics with Communists elsewhere in Europe who believe that the nation can fully and adequately control multinational enterprises. He denies that this is so, and adds that his party colleagues are of one mind on this point.

Italian Communists are careful to spell out that their proposals are not to be confused with older, antiquated, entirely unrealistic ideas of European integration that suggested that more of it would lead to less national sovereignty. Not only do they deny that the kinds of collaboration they propose would reduce national sovereignty, the Communists believe that it would actually increase it.

Communist Party leaders, therefore, emphasize that they favor greater collaboration among the trade unions of Western Europe; they want to create federations of left-wing parties in Western Europe; they want to strengthen the European Commission at Brussels, but only after direct election of members to the European Parliament has been arranged.

Communist leaders acknowledge that their efforts will not be easy. They know that left-wing parties in Europe are not of one mind about many policies, including how to treat the American presence there. They know, too, that a number of these parties fear what might appear to be an effort on the part of Italian Communists to achieve "homogenizing leadership" throughout Western Europe.

A further reason for international collaboration of the kind they have in mind is the opportunities that it would provide in the important sector of research and development. Communist respondents, as much as any other elites interviewed, acknowledge that there are a number of industrial sectors where neither Italy nor any other single European country acting alone can hope to be viable; so they want more international collaboration. In these sectors of very high technology, requiring enormous financial outlays and critical masses of intellectual and scientific power, they believe that the kind of nationalism that prevails in Europe is sheer folly.

About such nationalism, whether it occurs in the trade union or any other sphere, a major Communist leader says:

"It is absurd that the working class should be in a conservative and provincial posture that helps create a situation where countries like Italy wind up being squashed either by American or by Soviet hegemony. There must be developed a capacity to overcome single national egoisms."

Communist leaders take the view that the European Communities came into existence in part in response to needs of the United States in the era of the Cold War, in part in response to American capitalism's search for larger markets. With the advent of détente, they believe that one critical reason for adhering to the older conception of the European Community has been removed. Further, they point out that, while there is no necessary antagonism that should characterize American-European relationships, there is not any obvious commonality of interests either. They believe this point was made, but entirely too simplistically, by Servan-Schreiber some years ago. In any event, they support the idea that Europe should be an autonomous power center in its own right, and that this should imply dealing with both the United States and the Soviet Union on an arm's-length basis.

Because U.S. power in Europe is both symbolized and manifested by multinational enterprise, Communist leaders say it is natural that much attention should be focused there. This view is sometimes echoed by other Italian respondents, too. Clearly an important reason why so many Italians think that to be multinational means to be American is that the United States, as a nation-state, is so visible and so powerful in the international sphere. Some of the antagonism toward the American firm operating abroad, we are told, has much less to do with the issue of foreign ownership as such or with the overseas behavior of the multinational firm than it does with the basic fact that these firms are of American parentage.

One Communist respondent says that, in his view, the *only* nation in the world that today can fully control the multinationals—its own and those of other countries—is the United States. For this reason, he adds, greater collaboration among the nations of Europe "is the only way to combat the mischief created by fragmented nations and by multinationals operating within them."

In phrasing the Communist Party's most recent economic position cited above, Eugenio Peggio devotes several pages to the strategy described. He notes that Italy's need to be more autonomous and independent economically does not imply that it should "become closed within itself" or abandon the long-standing Italian policy of favoring international commercial and other forms of collaboration. "To be more autonomous does not mean to collaborate less. On the contrary." But Italy would make less of a real contribution to international comity than it should "if it should, in the name of collaboration, continue passively to submit to the arrogance of others." In these circumstances, the European Communities can do no less than completely revise their orientation and the basis on which their future collaboration can proceed. This implies new European policies regarding monetary exchange, energy, science and technology, the development of new markets, and a more open and active role in promoting relationships with the Socialist countries of the East.

Italian Communists say, then, that they are promoting a new form of political integration in Western Europe. The meaning of this, and some of its implications for the American firm operating abroad, are summed up in the following statement made by one of the PCI's leading figures:

"I do not mean that political integration would reduce the nation-state to a nullity. I do mean this: If little Italy decides to go it alone, the multinationals of the world—Italian or otherwise—will have her for breakfast. It is important that Europe move forward to confront . . . the problems and powers represented on the economic side by the multinationals.

"We want a new political understanding among European nations . . . so that the U.S. dollar does not command as predominantly as it once did. We require a situation where the United States does not define the rules of the game; indeed, we need new rules. If we do not reach agreement, . . . it's going to be much more difficult to deal with the multinationals."

Organizational Alternatives on Imperatives

Several interesting ideas about the future organization of the multinational enterprise emerge from this study. They can best be highlighted around the following questions: (1) Is the so-called multinational really multinational? (2) Is the multinational really a dinosaur? (3) Should the multinational be looking to new organizational forms?

Lawyers, scholars, and statesmen have filled rooms and volumes with words designed to provide an exact definition of what is—and what is not—a multinational enterprise. Such exchanges often lead to fine distinctions among business enterprises labeled, "multinational," "transnational" and "international." From time to time the distinctions and definitions find their way into catalogues.[5]

Are They Really Multinational?

Few of our respondents engage in definitional hairsplitting. But with remarkable frequency they do challenge the idea that American firms operating in Canada or Italy are "really" multinational. This is true of elites from every category. It is not merely Communists in Italy or nationalistic NDP members in Canada who see the American firm as no more than the extension abroad of the American parent company. Liberals and Conservatives, Christian Democrats and Republicans often share the same view.

Local business leaders and trade unionists say the same thing. Indeed, indigenous business leaders seem rather *more* likely than labor leaders to deny that U.S. firms operating in their countries are truly multinational.

A simple count of responses by Italians to the question of whether they identify "multinational enterprises" in fact with "*American* multinational enterprises"

---

[5] For one catalogue of definitions, see U.N., *Multinational Corporations in World Development*. ST/ECA/190, 1973, Annex II.

was done: of 39 replies, four people said that it depends on a variety of factors, twenty-one said yes, and fourteen said no. Of the fourteen who said no, four were academic economists and four were trade unionists. Those who responded positively, however, included large proportions of the government officials, political party leaders, and indigenous businessmen in the study.

In Canada, too, some trade union leaders tend to be more concerned with the phenomenon of the multinational in the world, especially the Third World, than with the specific impact of MNC's on Canada. But with the exception of some union leaders and some academic economists, the presence and impact in Canada of multinational enterprises refers to *American* enterprise.

Senior managers of the participating corporations in our study take much the same view. One of them, who has been a country chief executive officer and is now a regional director, says:

"The multinational corporations are not really multinational. They are national companies with units abroad. That is one reason why they are tainted wherever they go abroad."

Even those managers who refer to the multinationality of their firm wind up qualifying this idea. In more detailed discussion of operational issues they indicate that the companies are actually organized and operate fundamentally as branches or subsidiaries of the parent company.

Corporate executive respondents also say that the so-called *psychological* dimension that, according to some, helps to establish the degree of multinationality in a firm is largely a myth.[6] They refer to such things as the polycentric or geocentric perceptions or values of corporation managers, to the ability of these managers to integrate the idea of "dual citizenship"—to express loyalty both to one's home country and to the worldwide corporation in which one is an employee.

Managers consider these ideas to be largely the inventions of scholars and corporate mythmakers.[7] Italians and Canadians think of themselves essentially in national terms. That identity evidently maintains itself very well, even for those managers who spend a good deal of time away from their own countries.

The Americans met do not differ on this dimension. They distinguish themselves quite clearly from Canadians or Italians, who often are their own managerial colleagues in the same firm. Thus, if a developing sense of world corporate citizenship is a requirement of multinationality, most of the managers we interviewed show little sign of it.

This is not to say that most of our respondents in Italy or Canada think American

---

[6] See, for example, H. Perlmutter, "The Tortuous Evolution of the Multinational Corporation," *Columbia Journal of World Business* VI, January-February, 1969, pp. 9-18.

[7] See Robert L. Heilbroner, *Business Civilization in Decline*. New York: W.W. Norton & Co., Inc., 1976, pp. 91-2.

firms in their countries are the instruments of United States foreign policy. Some, of course, do, especially those on the political left. In some cases, as we showed earlier, this may be the most important perception of the U.S. firms that elites have. More of the elites—and more Canadians than Italians in this case—are angry that American firms permit themselves to be used for the extraterritorial application of U.S. law.

In any event, most of the Canadian and Italian elites in this study see the affiliate or subsidiary from the United States as essentially U.S. entities. Thus, they often write off the idea of multinationality as so much "nonsense." But if it is not "nonsense," elites say the idea of multinationality can be dangerous. The very last thing Canadian and Italian elites want is that firms be *more* multinational, if this implies that the firms will be even *less* responsive and responsible to host governments.

If U.S. firms with overseas operations cause certain problems, surely supranational firms that rise above all national sovereignties would cause many more. The elites assure us that U.S. business leaders, who believe that the kind of business organization that sees itself as a "citizen of the world" would be more attractive to host countries, are badly mistaken.

As things now stand, no one believes that American firms are really multinational. Even their indigenous managers overseas see themselves as carrying on essentially American overseas operations. As one Italian puts it: "Why would someone here think of himself as a multinational citizen when the only thing New York decentralizes is the dirty work for the local boys?"

Are They Dinosaurs?

If the multinational is not really multinational, is it, then, a dinosaur? An impressive number of Italian and Canadian respondents think so. They refer to size, scale and centralization. They have in mind the relationship between the size of the brain and the size of the body, where the brain is supposed to register what is going on everywhere in the environment and the anatomy, and to make intelligent adaptations and define necessary actions.

Much of what was noted earlier about the consequences of centralization is relevant here and does not require repeating. It is worth underlining once again, however, that in Canada at least the U.S. firms most favorably identified by Canadian elites as good corporate citizens are those that have the greatest amount of overall autonomy in relation to their respective parent companies. The point is that many of our respondents, including a surprising number of corporate managers, believe that size, scale and sensitivity are intimately related, in the long run, to survival. Therefore, they urge that more attention be paid to possible alternative organizational formats.

A number of individuals underline that the American MNC in its prevailing organizational format is very much the product of a particular historical era. Canadians and Italians say that American firms arrived in large numbers at a time when both countries had enormous needs for capital, technology and managerial skills, and when few of these resources were available locally. This situation was highly conducive to the formation of a certain type of international business organization, namely, the wholly owned subsidiary whose structure, mission, operating strategies, and other dimensions are tightly controlled from the center.

The international political situation of the era—from the late 1940's through the mid-1960's—further reinforced these organizational tendencies. During this period, the United States, Canada and West European governments created a three-cornered relationship, within which the community of U.S. multinational corporations flourished. These corporate structures provided basic support for carrying out essential tasks of postwar reconstruction, developing the western alliance, and stimulating western economic growth.[8]

That world no longer exists, and what was appropriate in it may not be appropriate in another. In fact, as it has been already shown this is a basic tenet of the Eurostrategy pursued by the Italian Communist Party. Canadians and Italians echo one another as they suggest some organizational alternatives that new times and new circumstances seem to dictate. They also articulate some intriguing differences.

Are New Organizational Forms Needed?

A number of our respondents, especially Italians, believe that the multinationals should consider the idea that "small is beautiful." Although the "small is beautiful" notion has many adherents in Canada, few of the Canadian elites we talked with feel that these ideas are particularly relevant to issues involving multinational organization. A surprising number of Italians, however, are strongly committed to the view that MNC's must develop much smaller units of production in the future. One Italian economist states that while the overall dimension of multinationals will grow with the expanded market, "the units of production are destined to get smaller." He continues: "In fact, the challenge and the problem for the multinational in the future is how to establish a better balance between man and society, and between them and their instruments."

Another Italian, a leading industrialist, says it is necessary "to encourage diversity, but real diversity." The multinational moves in the wrong direction at the present time: "The homogeneity that is imposed by monistic multinational structures is exactly what people do not want." Size is, in effect, identified with the remote, insensitive exercise of power, and with creating exactly the kind of environment that many people wish to avoid, or to change. And another economist says that he sees: "A clear tendency in Italy . . . a general tendency for large firms operating there to dismantle. . . . There is going to be a tendency to operate with smaller, perhaps more viable, economic units."

Italian trade unionists support this view. They note that, alongside the medium-sized plants in Italy, multinational firms seem less flexible, more cumbersome, less capable of reacting to certain adversities, or to capitalize on new oppor-

---

[8] See, for example, Robert Gilpin, U.S. Power and the Multinational Corporation. New York: Basic Books, 1975.

tunities. When they discuss the relative weight of absenteeism, social welfare payments, double employment, and so on, on large and small firms, the dinosaur image is compelling.

The reasons for this difference between Canadians and Italians are not entirely clear. One explanation for the greater interest in smaller units in Italy is, as the comment from a trade unionist suggests, "to escape some of the social and trade union pressures and costs that have now come into existence." Another may be the more generalized Italian reaction these days to the centralization of the state and its instruments. Italy, unlike Canada, is going through a period of wanting to regionalize and decentralize almost everything.

One Italian economist believes that "smaller scale multinationals" do better economically. As a result they are conspicuously absent from that subset of U.S. and other multinationals that are getting out. Canadians, on the other hand, are worried about enterprises that are too small. They feel the country suffers badly from the "miniature replica effect" in which too many firms produce too many products for the Canadian market.

Furthermore, whereas Italians are concerned about too much centralization within the country, Canadians worry about the strong centrifugal tendencies in the country. Many would like to encourage industrial organizations that are not only more efficient producers but are also instruments to help balance these strong decentralizing forces.

Canadians who talked about alternative forms of organization of multinational enterprises tend more to emphasize the creation of *larger-scale* but also more *autonomous* national units operating within the overall international MNC structure.

A former chief executive officer of a major U.S. firm in Canada describes three types of subsidiary: the "colonial international subsidiary," which is essentially a branch plant of the parent; the "integrated international subsidiary," which is one segment of a more truly multinational corporation in which worldwide research, production and marketing strategies are set by the parent; and the "commonwealth international affiliate," in which basic business strategies are set by the subsidiary management.

"The commonwealth relationship lets the subsidiary attain a high level of autonomy along with innovative design, production and marketing capability. Such opportunities may involve risk ventures to meet national needs that are competitive with undertakings in which the parent is engaged."[9]

Our Canadian respondents are quite clearly thinking in terms of the "commonwealth" model. The top managers of one subsidiary in our project are attempting to develop special product responsibilities, from research and development through to international marketing. They see the future of their company as a

[9] J. Herbert Smith, "FIRA's Obligation: Understand Parent, Subsidiary Relations," *Financial Times of Canada* (Toronto), May 3, 1976.

"Canadian-based multinational enterprise . . . linked by various ties to the American multinational parent." Their interest focuses strongly on developing internally competitive product lines and opening up their own export role. The chief executive officer of the firm says that "to rationalize productive structures in Canada will create units of production that are oversized for the Canadian market unless they have substantial international interests."

Another Canadian subsidiary manager group emphasizes the decentralization of research and development more than the development of an independent export role. What is important, they say, is to create a fully integrated organization within Canada that can be responsive to Canadian markets and to unique Canadian needs.

The federal concept comes up in several Italian interviews as well. One leading Italian industrialist emphasizes that to be small does not mean to give up certain advantages of scale. To be small means to be closer—even closer than most *nationally* independent but centralized structures can be—to the needs, demands and opportunities of a more geographically circumscribed environment. To be small in this sense means not merely decentralization, but the *devolution* of certain responsibilities to make decisions that seem right in a given territory.

Canadians seem to stress the importance of full-cycle activity by subsidiaries with worldwide responsibilities; and this view resonates in Italy. Italians stress as well the need for industrial decision making that will be closer to the devolution of policy-making powers to the regions that so many of them support, or say they desire.

The federal concept is considered novel in Italy, and not many Italians have much to say about it. One Italian who has, and who heads a major multinational corporation, describes how his organization "has taken great pains to create what can best be called a confederation, a confederal set of relationships among the operating units of the organization. To create this kind of structure requires that you make a more than superficial commitment to decentralization. It requires that you make more than a superficial commitment to the idea that what is good for the local company and the country in which it is operating will be good for the firm."

He adds that no firm can pretend to be multinational unless it can show convincingly that it is Italian in Italy, French in France, Brazilian in Brazil, and so on. In the long run, he says, even the federal imagery may imply too much central direction. We are talking about a future, he suggests, where confederations—or consortia—of national firms share and exploit certain advantages that the association itself produces.

Some of our respondents go beyond these organizational ideas to reflect on quite radical alternatives to what now exists. A top executive in an American parent firm wonders whether his company, if it could do it all over, would go abroad knowing the world would come to look as it does today. A country manager in Italy, whose parent firm has experienced one overseas disaster after another (based, he says, on a total misreading of overseas political trends), is certain that the top managers of his company would vote to stay at home.

A Canadian manager says it may be better to sell technology and license overseas production than to be directly involved. A leading Italian statesman suggests that what we will find around the corner of time is the "mini-multinational." Some he says are already in existence: "They buy technologies and then rent them out in exchange for royalties." These multinationals, he believes, are not as visible as those we are accustomed to. They cannot as readily be associated with fears of political interference, or with the greater fear that powers beyond the nation exercise elusive economic powers over the host country.

Possible Response Alternatives

In the next five or ten years, a most critical issue will be whether U.S. firms can respond to new demands and policies abroad, and what form of corporate organization and decision making this response will take. A necessary condition for creative and fruitful adaptation will be that the firms have a clearer understanding of the goals, values and patterns of political and social change in host countries. While there is time to develop these skills, there is very little time to waste in doing so.

This is not an easy recommendation to implement. In several firms we found that such analysis was lacking not because senior managers were unaware of the need for it, but because they feel the task poses insurmountable difficulties. It is this presupposition that must be modified before reticence can be overcome. In the process of reaching in this direction, a number of caveats will be in order.

First, as noted above, political analysis should describe probable alternatives and the decisional options that may go with them. Such analysis will illuminate conflicting interests, goals and strategies assumed by relevant actors and organizations. It will separate political hunches, fantasies and fears about the future from roughly probable and improbable patterns of development.

Second, analyses will tend to be shaped in some measure by the perspective and predispositions of the analysts. Political analysts do not differ from economic analysts on this score.

Third, analyses carried out by U.S. subsidiaries may differ quite substantially from those carried out by the parent company. Understanding the reasons and the import of such discrepancies is part and parcel of the more sophisticated kind of analysis.

Fourth, as often in the case of economic analysis, an array of charts, tables and numbers can give the senior executive a false sense of confidence in the data and recommendations that accompany them.

Finally, one wants to recognize that initial attempts at this type of analysis will probably not live up to expectations. In these circumstances, as we learned about one of our participating firms, the entire enterprise may be abandoned. A more appropriate response, we believe, would be to try to improve the analysis.

And this is an appropriate note on which to conclude this report. The evidence is very strong that problems for American firms overseas cannot easily be divorced from problems that confront the United States as a major world power. In its most typical contemporary organizational format, the U.S. multinational looks overpoweringly American, in the political as well as the economic sense. Many of the people we interviewed in Italy and Canada, including many managers of U.S.

firms in those countries, suggest that it is now time for those who head U.S. multinational corporations to rethink some of these issues—not only those involving basic MNC organizational format, but the others touched upon in this report.

Appendix
The Problem and Its Setting

The Problem

The problem posed for this study was: what conditions and affects the conduct of American corporate enterprise abroad, where the enterprise itself is in the form of direct investment. The problem can be restated in many ways, and can easily be made to encompass the widely voiced concerns about "social responsibility" and "good corporate citizenship." A great deal of public, governmental and scholarly attention has centered recently on the multinational corporation as an institution. The behavior, or alleged misbehavior, the influence and impact (good or bad) of the multinational corporation writ large has come under intense scrutiny. It is this institution—often treated as a single undifferentiated category—that excites fear or polemics, acrimonious debate on or demands for greater national and international controls of the institution itself.

Propositions about Corporate Citizenship and Management

We begin with the self-evident proposition that, whatever may be the ambitions or motivations of corporate managers, they are never in complete control of the factors that affect their business activities at home or abroad. We assume that these managers must pay attention to the "bottom line," but also that they understand this constraint is not always, or even necessarily, at odds with the idea of "good corporate citizenship."

We also assume that "good corporate citizenship" and "social responsibility" are not understood to mean the same thing in all countries, or even in a single country at different times in its economic, social and political history. Moreover, we assume that *any* given corporate commitment to a particular mode or style of business abroad will encounter approbation *and* criticism, support *and* opposition in host countries.

These assumptions, if they are reasonable, lead to a second proposition, namely, that there will always be points of tension between those who manage corporate subsidiaries abroad and certain individuals, groups and organizations that are indigenous to the host countries. Understanding the nature of these points of tension, their underlying causes, is a first step toward establishing the *requirements* and the *limits* of "socially responsible" American corporate behavior abroad. In the limiting cases, it is these points of tension that will determine whether direct foreign investment abroad will be desired by investors or permitted by host countries.

Environmental Variables

The factors or variables that might impinge on the American corporate presence overseas run a very wide gamut. Many of these are strictly economic; large-scale corporations have a wealth of knowledge of and experience with these areas. Furthermore, an extensive literature is now available, dealing with negotiations pertaining to the establishment of overseas operations; fiscal, financial and monetary aspects of such operations; problems of credit and finance, development and adaptation of new product lines, the opening and exploitation of new markets, and so on.[1] We do not treat such factors in this study.

We are greatly concerned here with certain *political* and *social* structural variables that deeply affect American multinational enterprise abroad. Political factors are often parametric, that is, they set fairly rigid limits within which business enterprise abroad can proceed. The most obvious of these factors, of course, is a given nation's public policies and regulations regarding the presence of foreign capital in the economy. This reality is less apparent in countries whose policies regarding foreign investment are liberal and encouraging than in places where such economic inputs are carefully scrutinized and severely controlled. As national governments at home and abroad become more restive about "multinationals," the relevance of political variables becomes more apparent to all.

Public policies affecting multinational coporations are largely the result of interactions among a nation's "strategic elites."[2] Certain members of this group will be responsible for how effectively such policies are implemented or executed. These policies, it must be added, are not merely those found in host countries where U.S. firms may be located; they involve as well those policies of the United States government that directly or indirectly pertain to the overseas operations of U.S. companies.

On the social variable side, one could name a large number of specific items that condition U.S. corporate behavior in host countries. Deeply rooted modes of work and leisure, relationships between employers and employees, connections between familial, educational and economic institutions are examples of such items. Inadequate understanding of these and similiar things on the part of corporate managers can often create avoidable problems.

Corporate Citizenship Definitions

Because social mores do vary a good deal, we hypothesize that definitions of good corporate citizenship produced in the United States will not necessarily appeal, or be acceptable, to persons abroad. This elementary but important insight tends to be obscured when newspapers, lawmakers, the general public, scholars and corporate executives themselves fail to distinguish, for example, between bribery and extortion, or fail to acknowledge that there does not exist a single, universal moral code that applies to the behavior of those who manage economic enterprises.

Operationalizing Elite Interviews

The principal social structural variable of concern to us in this study refers to the strategic elites of host countries. We hold that it is the perceptions, attitudes,

---

[1] See, for example: F. Machlup, W.S. Salant and L. Tarshis (eds.), *International Mobility and Movement of Capital.* New York: Columbia University Press, 1972; M.Z. Brooke and H.L. Renners, *The Strategy of Multinational Enterprise: Organization and Finance.* London: Longmans, 1971; C.P. Kindelberger (ed.), *The International Corporation: A Symposium.* Cambridge, Mass.: M.I.T. Press, 1970; S. Rolfe and W. Damm (eds.), *The Multinational Corporation in the World Economy.* New York: Praeger, 1970; J.W. Stopford and L.T. Wells, *Managing Multinational Enterprises: Organization of the Firm and Ownership of the Subsidiaries.* New York: Basic Books, 1972; D.B. Zenoff and J. Zwick, *International Financial Management.* Englewood Cliffs, N.J.: Prentice-Hall, 1969.

[2] The concept of "strategic elites" is delineated in depth by Suzanne Keller, *Beyond the Ruling Class: Strategic Elites in Modern Society.* New York: Random House, 1963.

expectations and demands of these elites, as these refer to foreign investment and multinationals, that primarily define the limits of corporate behavior within host countries. We do not wish entirely to ignore the role of public opinion in this matter, but assign it a secondary role. At best, "public opinion" is a manipulated and instrumental factor, reflecting interactions among elites and certain (sometimes volatile) relationships between elites and the public.[3]

We therefore concentrate our attention on those in a host country whose opinions, attitudes, expectations and demands count more significantly. We sought a set of respondents who, by reason of the positions they occupy and/or the influence they can wield, can and do make a substantial difference in the affairs of foreign companies in their midst. We hypothesized, among other things, that persons who fit this description in most nation-states (but particularly in nation-states with their own multinational corporations) do *not* in general fear multinational corporations. Nor do they ascribe to them the kinds of powers or acts of uncontrolled or uncontrollable misbehavior one reads and hears about these days.

Strategic Elites in Host Countries

Of prime importance to us among the strategic elites of host countries were persons defined by Lindblom as "proximate decision makers."[4] These are persons so intimately involved in the machinery of public policymaking that their acts of commission or omission can be shown to have a direct impact on the determination and execution of such policies. Legislators, cabinet members, highest-level public administrators and judges are in this category. Others are a step or two removed from these formal "levers of power," but they are nevertheless significant: Leading trade unionists and industrialists, mass media representatives, economists and intellectuals fall into this category. In general, we were after a very special subset of what Italians call the "political class."

The categories of strategic elites from which the subset would be drawn are relatively easy to identify. Cabinet members; lawmakers; civil and military administrators; trade union, industrial association, and other interest-group leaders; members of the indigenous business and banking communities; economists, academics and intellectuals; mass media leaders; strategically placed regional and local personalities—all of these constitute a listing of the categories we employed.

Within these categories we did not attempt probability or random sampling, for many reasons. In most instances no complete enumeration of those to be included in the universe to be sampled was possible. Our financial resources permitted in-depth, focused interviews with a limited number (75-100) of persons per country; probability sampling by category would have been pretentious under these circumstances. More important, however, was our judgment that concentrating on "proximate decision makers" required making every reasonable effort, within each category utilized, to identify those who weigh more importantly than others regarding the central problem explored.

---

[3] This point of view is spelled out at length in Joseph LaPalombara, *Politics Within Nations*. Englewood Cliffs, N.J.: Prentice-Hall, 1974, Ch. 9. For a sustained analysis of the utilities to be derived from research that centers on political elites, see Robert Putnam, *The Comparative Study of Political Elites*. Englewood Cliffs, N.J.: Prentice-Hall, 1976.

[4] See C.E. Lindblom, *The Policy-Making Process*. Englewood Cliffs, N.J.: Prentice-Hall, 1968.

Thus, not just any cabinet minister would do. We tried to identify present or former ministers of industry, or the treasury, or those in a ministry of foreign affairs whose formal responsibilities require them to be in contact with or to know something about multinational corporations. The same consideration was applied to trade union leaders, economists, newspaper editors, party leaders, and others who constitute our "sample" of elites. We wanted persons at the very top who, wherever possible, should also be those knowledgeable about and able to affect policies toward multinationals.

Technically speaking, we utilized primarily the "positional method" for identifying those to be interviewed. This core group in each country was supplemented by approximately an additional 15 percent, who were elites identified by the "reputational method."[5] Within each category we were able to interview relatively few persons.

U.S. Officials and Managers of U.S. MNC's

Beyond the strategic elites of host countries, two other categories of respondents were of interest to us. First, we interviewed representatives of the U.S. government, at home or in the host countries selected, who know something about and/or maintain relationships with American multinational corporations, or who have specific responsibilities regarding the host countries of the study. Among other things, we needed such respondents in order to test the hypothesis that, both at home and abroad, communications between representatives of business and government are minimal; where such communications do exist, they rarely pertain in a meaningful way to the problem of this study.

Managers of U.S. multinationals in parent or regional headquarters, and in the company affiliates located in host countries, constitute the second additional category of respondents. Beyond factors overseas that can and do affect corporate operations, the organizational features of the multinational firm will also affect the behavior of the firm's overseas affiliate. We were interested in exploring how such behavior is affected by: (1) patterns of recruitment and mobility to managerial positions; (2) the degree and kind of decentralization of decisional authority involved; (3) size and age of the overseas affiliate; (4) the quality of overseas managerial personnel; (5) assessments of existing organizational arrangements by headquarters, regional and local managers; and (6) patterns of information gathering, reporting and information utilization in decisions.

In particular, we hypothesized that the "success" of a corporate overseas operation will vary with the extent to which in-depth information of a socio-political (as opposed to strictly economic or financial) nature is generated and utilized by corporate decision makers with responsibilities for overseas operations.

Choice of Firms

A few overseas managers of American firms were included in our interviews as a result of selection procedures followed abroad. However, in order to maximize the comparability of our country data, and the authenticity of our information

---

[5] The technical meaning of various methods of selecting elites as a source of primary data in social research is discussed by LaPalombara, 1974.

about corporations themselves, we found it essential to secure the collaboration of U.S. firms.

Ten U.S. multinational corporations cooperated in this study. All of them (of varying size and overseas experience) are involved in processing, fabrication, assembly and marketing activities in the countries studied. The companies represent only five industrial sectors: chemicals, automotive, pharmaceuticals, hydrocarbons, and electric and electronic products. In all but the automotive category, affiliates of the firms exist in both countries that constitute the research sites. Corporate managers in the parent companies, in regional European offices where they exist, and in the host-country affiliates were interviewed. In many instances, these managers were interviewed two or three times.

Choice of Host Countries

A number of criteria underlie the choice of countries. For example, we decided that in this phase of the research we would limit our activity to countries that are "Western" and industrial. In a second phase, research will also be conducted in several Third World countries, but even there we will be interested in criteria of selection such as the following:

(1) The *distribution by country of the total sum of American direct investment abroad.* On this criterion, for example, Canada and Britain are in a separate category, accounting for approximately 36 percent of U.S. investment in 1973. One of these two countries, on this criterion alone, was attractive to us as a research site.

(2) The *relative weight of U.S. investment* in the total economy. Canada, again, has a very special status here. If any nation-state conforms to what some writers intend by "dependency theory," Canada should be that place. We were also mindful that Canada, like Mexico, borders the United States but nevertheless remains one of the countries of the world which to date has been least studied by U.S. scholars.

(3) The *diversity* of U.S. direct investment in the host country. We wished to avoid in the first place countries where U.S. investment is large and weighs heavily on the local economy *but* is concentrated in a single economic sector, such as the extractive industries. Canada and Italy provide settings for a rich variety of U.S. multinational investment. Over seven hundred U.S. firms in Italy, and in excess of two thousand such firms in Canada, provide local experiences with U.S. firms, and perceptions of them, that are not distorted by multinational concentration in one sector, or local experiences with only a handful of the most prominent U.S. firms.

(4) The *degree of public attention* to the presence of U.S. firms in the host country. For reasons that become abundantly plain in our report, Canadians have generated intense, almost obsessive, concern with the presence of U.S. capital in their country. The "psychology of dependency" one encounters there tends to center on the U.S. corporate subsidiary. In recent months, Italy has also generated intense, widely diffused and publicized interest in multinationals. The reason for all of this interest is not so much the presence there of U.S. (and other foreign) firms but, rather, *corporate* decisions to get out. In addition, the prospect

that the Italian Communists may come to share political power in Italy made it a country of prime interest to us.

In addition, Italy and Canada have achieved recent prominence as countries where large-scale corporate payments, of a more or less acceptable and/or legal nature, have occurred. However, these events escalated *after* the two countries were chosen as research sites.

(5) The *potential typicality* of the country from the vantage point of problems confronting U.S. firms operating there. Canada struck us as the forerunner of countries establishing public policies and organizations designed to bring about more self-conscious regulation and control of foreign investment. Indeed, our field work revealed that Italians are looking intensively at Canada as a model to be followed (or improved upon) in this important regard.

Italy also seems to have great potential for being "typical" along a variety of relevant dimensions, several of which are discussed in detail in this report. These include patterns of industrial relations, growing demands for new forms of equity sharing, relations between private and public industrial sectors, and systems of administered prices. In addition, the Italian trade unions and left wing political parties are spearheading an effort to bring about a Europeanwide strategy pertaining to multinational enterprises. It seemed highly attractive to learn about this "Eurostrategy" in detail from those persons and organizations who are its major spokesmen and architects.

(6) The *prevailing policies* toward direct foreign investment. Canada and Italy, as we detail in the study, have been quite similar in the degree of openness and liberality they have extended to those interested in direct foreign investment in the local economies. This historical receptivity, coupled with growing concern about foreign investment and demands for more self-conscious public policies regarding it, suggested a baseline condition of similarity that would facilitate useful comparisons between the two countries.

No single country, or pair of countries, can fully "represent" the diversity of local conditions that affect foreign enterprises operating abroad. We opted for a micro-level approach to this problem, as opposed to securing less useful—or empirically unverified—information on large numbers of countries or corporations. We assume that more micro-level studies, focusing on single countries and a limited number of firms, will be required before we can separate what is valid or invalid about the avalanche of theories, claims, charges, hunches, ideas and fantasies people have had about the operations of the multinational firm outside its home country.

Conduct of Interviews

The total number of interviews conducted in the United States, Canada, Italy and European regional headquarters is 190. These interviews sometimes involved more than a single respondent; thus, the total number of participants in these interviews is 247 (see Table A-1).

The field work was conducted between December 1975, and June, 1976. Canadian interviews were conducted by Stephen Blank, assisted by Elizabeth Hanson. All Italian interviews were conducted by Joseph LaPalombara during December, 1975-January, 1976 and May-June, 1976.

Table A-1: Interviews and Respondents by Category of Respondent and Locus of Interview

Interviews with U.S.Government officials in:	Interviews	Individuals
Washington	7	14
Italy	4	5
Canada	1	5
Local elites and opinion leaders in:		
Italy	62	68
Canada	51	67
Managers of cooperating corporations in:		
The United States	16	25
Italy	16	16
Canada	26	38
Europe	7	9
Total	190	247

In both Canada and Italy a number of the national elites interviewed held more than one position. This often made them highly relevant and they appear in more than one of the elite categories of interest to us. For example, a trade union leader, who is also a member of parliament and a political party leader, would fit at least two categories. A matrix depicting the distribution of our respondents by category of elite, with some respondents counted twice, appears in Table A-2.

An unusual opportunity to try out some of our earliest analytical impressions was afforded by a meeting held in May, 1976, with approximately thirty middle- and top-level managers of the FIAT Corporation. These men and women were pointed in their reactions to our findings, and illuminating in expressing their own attitudes toward American multinational firms—often their competitors at home and abroad. On the whole, their remarks helped to persuade us that our methodology is correct and our Italian findings are representative and valid.

Table A-2: Distribution of Canadian and Italian Elite Respondents, by Category of Elite Status*

	Canada	Italy
Ministers (national, provincial, past, present)	5	5
Political Party Leaders (national)	2	18
National Bureaucrats	16	7
Provincial Party or Bureaucratic Elites	12	3
Indigenous Business Leaders	16	17
Managers of Collaborating Corporations	38	16
Labor Leaders	3	8
Mass Media	3	10
Intellectuals, Academics, Researchers	15	20
Economists	10	10

* Some individuals are counted in two categories